Fractures and Echoes
An Anthology in Being

by Coninyah B. Dew and *The Teacher*

DORRANCE
PUBLISHING CO
EST. 1920
PITTSBURGH, PENNSYLVANIA 15238

Dorrance Publishing Co
585 Alpha Drive
Pittsburgh, PA 15238
Visit our website at *www.dorrancebookstore.com*

ISBN: 979-8-89027-336-9
eISBN: 979-8-89027-834-0

Fractures and Echoes

An Anthology in Being

Introduction

Thank you for allowing me the honor and privilege to share my story with you. I spent many years running and hiding from my own insecurities. It wasn't until I had a friend share with me a book he was reading that my life took on a trajectory of sincere seeking. He, and I to a greater extent, was unaware that his actions set me on a path to find my *Teacher*. I consumed author after author to find the answers to questions that had nagged me well before I even knew of their existence. Each author came to me at very pivotal times in my life that helped me to get a step further. My process was clunky, undisciplined, and varied in its outcomes. Through my continued inquiry, *Teachers* in my everyday life manifested rather than just on the pages of the books I read. The *Teachers* took me from the intellectual to the experiential. It is in the experiential that I began my true work in examining my life and the lessons I learned along the way. I do not profess to have THE ANSWER. Rather, this book is designed to share with you through my experiences what I have learned and provide a glimpse of how this work continues to be living and breathing in my everyday life.

The nature of exploring and engaging in my life is never ending. It is my hope the same is true for you. We can easily fall into patterns of repetition and not consider if we are living our fullest selves. Through mindful practices and moments of reflections, we may get closer to understanding what it is we are to be doing in our lives to live our sacred purpose. I am guilty of having been in moments of dead spots in my life where I experienced numbness, anger, and aimlessness. I have been guilty of lashing out and not understanding why I did not have the certainty of careers, of family, or of places to build my life that I saw in my own contemporaries. I came to understand each of our journeys is different. The entries are personal, and at the time of their writing, may not have been shared with all those who were the players in that story. I acknowledge the entries may sit unwell with some, and it is only through the intention of healing that these stories are shared.

I was guided to write this book through many unsolicited nudges as my signposts. We each may have signposts to guide us to the next step. That next step may not provide clarity in the moment as to how that step added to the foundation we were building. It is through reflection that those steps and their contributions may be brought into greater focus. This book was written in a way that allows each entry to stand alone. The single-entry page format was done to enable readers to sit with a single entry or with multiple at a time. There is not a fluid story that would tie each entry together seamlessly. They are individual moments that have added to my lived experiences.

Some readers may choose to journey from the start and travel to the last pages as they are presented. Others may choose to engage with the entries as they are called to do so which may mean opening the book to a random entry and allowing it to speak to you as it will. My hope is, no matter the choice of engagement, the words contained within will serve you. It is my wish that they bring about remembering, reacquainting, with your own life's experiences. Those moments that may have appeared inconsequential at the time may have shaped and molded who you have come to be. Equally they may have not garnered your attention until this moment. This is my gift. May my stories inspire you to examine yours and to share with others all you have learned. Shall we begin?

A Note to the Reader

Each passage may have words, phrases, or full texts italicized. Equally there may be words capitalized counter to grammatical rules. All has been written with intention. I invite you to reflect upon the intention and to draw your own conclusions regarding why they deserve the emphasis given to them. Of note, blank space is provided at the end of each entry for you to capture your own personal reflections. Happy journeying.

Dear *Teacher*,

Much of my life has felt as though I have not had awareness of my sacred purpose. There have been moments, sparks of direction and inspiration propped only by extensions of drought and fogs in clarity. I know, to my core, I am to serve and to support the *light* shining wherever I find myself. My struggle is in how to do *Your* asking and still feel the blessings and joys of my human experience. How do I continue on with simply being and resolving the voice I hear that tells me I am to do and be so much more? It is in this space I feel the sadness anchored in the certainty that all will be alright in time. Though, human time and *Your* time, my *Teacher*, are far different. I sit, I pray, I listen and still I am shaded in the shadows. *Your* guiding messages come in many forms: the wind through the pines, the Eagle's screech, the child's hurt and cry, the whisper of an innocent passerby. Each seems to know the message they carry, and I do not have the translations.

Young One, you hear, feel and sense My presence, My messages, love, care and protection I have shared with you with each waking breath, with each act of kindness, with each prayer of gratitude. You say you are shrouded in the shadows. What have those moments taught you?

They have taught me to quiet, to settle, to open to the vibrations of that which is *universal*, so they shine their *light* where there is none. Those moments have taught me patience, compassion and the wisdom that comes with holding both the shadows and the inspirations sacred.

And what of the sadness and grief?

They have shared they each are a gift that alight the depths of my compassion and love I have to share. When my compassion and love have no vehicle for expression, the darkness sets in. The sparks and embers dim close to being extinguished.

And what keeps them alive?

It is remembering my hope, my trust and my deep knowing that my life, my experiences, my expression — matters.

And how do you keep that knowing alive and vital in your everyday experience?

I do so by listening and expressing my compassion and love in the ways I have relied on and in ways I have yet to discover.

My dearest *Teacher*, I raise my hands in gratitude, my voice of praise for *Your* lessons. In this moment and every moment hereafter, my commitment, my contract with *You* is to keep going. My word mandates I share what I am able so that others may also know their compass and their direction and their *light*.

Dear *Teacher*,

Many human years, moon cycles and changes in seasons have passed since my youth. My sensitivities to the hurts, the pains of my own and that of others, held me quiet in my thoughts and voice. I retreated deep into the realms spoken only of in stories and tales. In those worlds, I played, and I laughed. I made friends who promised my safety in return for my loyalty. Each time I returned to the waking world, I was reminded such worlds exist only in my experience untethered to that which is real. And slowly I forgot. I forgot how to play. I forgot how to dream. I forgot how to hold all experiences with inquiry, with wonder, with awe.

What was the cost of you forgetting?

I lost my memories of that time. I lost the comforts of the unseen and the knowledge of languages beyond that of the human world. The cost was my innocence, my laughter and my joy in the smallest of experiences.

What were the gifts in forgetting?

I learned to survive in a world that does not value fantasy or sensitivity to the pains not visible or palpable to the everyday experiences of others. I learned to stand in my own strength. I learned to rebuild my capacity for bringing humor to even the most emotionally crippling of experiences. I learned to shield my compassion and love, tucking them away so they may be nurtured to grow in their fullness. I learned the unseen worlds are always with me in my faith and in my trust.

And what of your childhood?

It lives while reminding me, through my *magical one*, he is, I am, a part of the *creative* experience. What I will with my thoughts, my words and my actions yield the blossoms of those efforts. My childhood reminds me of the deep beliefs I hold will guide my work, my engagements and my view of the world around me. Should anger and judgment be my azimuths, the world around me shall reflect that deep *truth* I hold. Should compassion and love be my guideposts, my world will hold me, similarly, in that *truth*.

In this moment, I have offered nothing more than a space for your reflection. For now, I leave you with this message: we are born, we grow, we mature and if we are lucky, we die with grace and dignity. Your work is not yet done. Your lessons are not all yet learned. Return to this space of communion often so that we may continue your learning.

Dear *Teacher,*

Long before my conception, long before my ability to walk or to talk, long before my self-awareness, bestowed upon me was the *warrior spirit* and the legacies of my ancestors who birthed, carried and embodied that way of being. I donned the uniform and carried arms not understanding doing so was but an aspect of the *warrior spirit*. The conflict I felt in the possibility of ending another life to save my own, or that of another, ruptured my identity tied intimately to the armed forces. My definition of the *warrior spirit* was forced to expand. The likes of Maya Angelou, The Rainbow Warriors, Desmond Tutu and many others, informed that expansion.

Why were they warriors who embodied the warrior spirit?

They each stood in their alignment with their sacred purposes while unyielding to the whims of human emotions or the dictates of others for how and who to be. They held to their right to be, their right to full self-expression, their right to learn, their right to grow and their right to celebrate their lives.

What do their examples say of the warrior spirit?

The *warrior spirit* is carried in each of us. It drives us in the cycles of life and death and holds us accountable to our *Creator(s)* to fully actualize who and what we were born to be.

How will you choose to live the warrior spirit?

I choose to do no harm to all things to the best of my ability. I choose to give gratitude and thanks for my lessons and forgive when I must do harm in protecting my life and safety and that of others. I will pass on what I have learned in the way of resolving the hurts. I will live with my heart open, with my *spirit* expanding and with my doings as my legacy.

Doing so is the way of honoring the warrior spirit. With these intentions, the circles of completion and wholeness are held in integrity. The complete circles of wholeness touch and share with other circles and with other warrior spirits committed to passing on a better world.

Thank you, dearest *Teacher*. I wish only to continue my learning and holding the *warrior spirit* in my life's cadence.

Young One,

I invite you now to contemplate your dreaming. You spoke of your lost connection to the fantastical worlds during your maturation. By reason, where did your dreaming go?

My *dreaming* went the way of the fantastical worlds into my forgetting. Each day I woke remembering only the shadows of the dark, the black screens of nothingness. I questioned many times why I did not dream, and if I did, where did they go upon waking.

What were your conclusions?

I was made aware through the times of quiet *reflection* that there are many parts to my being. My mind, both the creative and the analytical, my body in its physical and subtle forms, my spirit, my emotions and my subconscious all hold their different agendas. Their agendas were often at odds. In the fray was my *dreaming* as a casualty only showing itself with great trauma. And so, I stopped listening. I stopped showing care for my *dreaming* as also a part of me, and the conflict of my parts continued on.

Imprisoned by your neglect, how did your dreaming respond?

My *dreaming* grew impatient and demanded my attention. With subtle cracks in my guards, dreams of joy and comfort touched my awareness. I dismissed those moments as exceptions to the vast fields of darkness and nightmares. Yet my *dreaming* persisted.

How so?

My *dreaming* was to be the *bridge* between all of my parts of my inner world and the intersection with the waking world. My *dreaming* petitioned my mind, and out of that alliance grew my curiosity. I began to question the darkness, the nightmares, their terror, and why they were so voluminous. I began to learn they were warnings, nudges, to facilitate my healing and to keep me safe not only in my dreams but also in my waking world. As I listened more, questioned more, the nightmares eased. The screens of my *dreaming* began to populate with all sorts of images and fantasies. I began experiencing with all aspects of my emotions, not just my fear.

What more did you learn of your dreaming?

I learned my *dreaming* is very much living, breathing and expands beyond my sleep. My *dreaming* is felt in my daydreams, in the divine nods of coincidence and as a part of the greater fabric of the *Greater Dreaming*.

Much gratitude and thanks to you, my *Teacher*, for your continued support and guidance.

Dear *Teacher*,

In my reflections, I am reminded of the history of my pain, my loneliness and my questions of self-worth. I would lie in my room deep in my isolation, curtains drawn, blankets covering my head where no *light* was able to shine. Even during the day, the *light* of the sun was dim. Time slowed as I lived in that place of hurt. My tears burned and flowed as though never ending. My heart cried out, aching to be held, to be understood and to be kept safe. Where were *You?*

Young One, I felt your pain as you cried laying feeling abandoned. I heard your pleas. And, I had to honor your free will. Though your heart ached, there was a deeper longing to know sorrow as your teacher.

My *Teacher*, respectfully, I do not understand. *You* have said I chose to know sorrow. Why would my heart's longing have made such a choice? Why would I choose to experience such levels of darkness? Why would I choose pain?

How else would you have learned compassion? How else would you have learned its gifts? How else would you have come to know of your capacities to grow, to build your faith and trust in the process and the natural order of all things?

Each hurt and joy has its lessons. That is the blessing and wisdom of experience. Only once when you were able to learn the lesson sorrow had for you was I able to be felt in your life, in your hopes and in your dreams.

I hear your silence. Where have your thoughts taken you in this moment?

I sense the *truth* of your counsel. Yet, I struggle in accepting that I, in some way, brought about my circumstances that would manifest such hurts.

You have misunderstood. You are but a part of creating or, be it, attracting your circumstances. Your life is touched and influenced by the natural order and, equally, by chance.

That is too difficult for me to accept. I am left with many more questions than answers.

Be now with your questions. Allow them to form, to live in the spaces of quiet. When you are ready, I will be here as I have always been for and with you.

Dear *Teacher,*

The time has passed and with it, many reflections. The last we communed, I was left with countless questions. I confess I have yet to discover all those I feel stirring. Although, from this time of quiet, I have remembered the lifeline that helped me continue through my times of sorrow.

Please continue. What have you discovered?

I discovered there are many gates, accesses, to *that which moves and inspires all* in our external and internal worlds. For some it is through the culinary arts. For others, it is through playing in the natural world far from the concrete and structures that touch the skies. For others it is through service. For me, my access was and is through music. Music held me in her rhythms of change and those of hope. She reminded me there is a rhythm to all things, and each of us has our own rhythm. It is our individual rhythms that dance with the *universal rhythm* bringing into being the sacred songs of creation and change.

How did your lifeline in music save you?

She was my nurturer, my comforter, my healer. She moved my emotions and my body, reminding me of the blessings of my life itself.

And where was I?

You were inviting me to dance the rhythms of the *universe* through constantly whispering in the songs, in the movements. I had no words but only the know-ing. It was in the music that I would find my way. I would find my way to *You.* *And what of the darkness and sorrow during those times?*

The music now reminds me they were never total and complete so long as I shared the fullness of my pain with music. She would hold me steady until I was once more able to stand fully in the *light*.

You have done well. Your gate to the universal rhythm is not just through that of sound and music as you have come to discover. Though that is true, how has reconnecting with the universal rhythm sustained — saved — you?

I recognize that place of connection as my parts settle and the internal conflicts quiet. I feel safe in my own being. I feel whole in those moments unbound by human judgments of who and what I should be. I feel right as I am in alignment with the *universal rhythm*.

What then is the lesson?

The lesson is to return to those gates often. It is with that *universal rhythm* that I have the clarity, the courage and the strength to *be*.

Dear *Teacher*,

Looking back through my time of growth, I can't help but feel some regrets for hopes and wishes unrealized. In my insecurities, I bowed to my fears and to the poisonous beliefs of doubt. I perceived the choices I made as safe ones. I chose not to pursue medicine. I chose not to reconnect with lost, familial relationships. I chose not to have my own children for fear of bearing that responsibility alone and, thus, feeling the pain of not sharing my love in ways known only by that of a mother or father. Why in my adult life are my fears so strong? How do I overcome these fears to hold at bay future manifestations of regrets and to resolve those of my past?

Young One, your fear is a very real emotion. In balance, your fear keeps you safe when faced with real, physical dangers. When imbalanced, your fear paralyzes; it stirs in you; it forces you to run from your very own shadow. Overcoming your pattern of fear, paralysis and regret begins with inquiry. Ask whether your fear is being charged by real danger or by the imaginings of your creative mind. If real, follow your fear's lead. If not, thank your fear, breath, leap and explore the unknown.

I shared sorrow has the power to teach. Regret, equally, has its own wisdom if we are willing to hear its message. Be still. What is its message for you?

Not having my own children enabled me to attend to my own healing of hurts birthed by my childhood longing and absence of my own father. I was taught to know that pain and to share the knowledge, through my life's example, of how to survive. I learned I adore children, their innocence and their laughter. I adore their unfettered experimentation and play in the world. I learned to acknowledge each child needs nurturance and fostering, which have many forms. Through my teaching, I share with many young ones and encourage them in the ways I am able.

Beyond food, shelter and clothing as the means of nurturance and fostering, what more do children need?

Safety. I learned my will to keep a child safe is born of my own experience and contract with my inner child. I am a part of a greater consciousness committed to fostering the protection and *safety* of the young.

And what teaching, then, has your regret shared?

My regret has shown me it is a window and a bridge between what was, what could have been and what is. The trio, when carried together, houses wisdom and honors regret as another of my teachers.

Dear *Teacher,*

Families and their makeup have changed in my observations, but the dynamics within them have not. Families play, fight, avoid and incite many roleplays consistent with each member's position within the family. The father may withhold affection because he has not made a kinship with his own emotional body. He may misperceive emotion as weakness and an affront to his masculinity. The daughter may feign helplessness to avoid responsibility for her own power and strength. The brother may be always the one looked to as fortunate in all he does; yet, he is unable to achieve the self-image of perfection he is beholden to within his family. And still, the mother may always be the nurturer at the cost of her own wellbeing; or opposite, she may be demanding at the risk of the nurturance of the family. I was the quiet son and brother to never make a fuss though I would scream inside, "Hear me!"

When I find myself among my family, I regress to those roles I held. Those roles and expectations run contrary to the person I have come to know as my true *being*. Why is it that we regress to old patterns, likened to ill-fitted clothing, that no longer present who we are or choose to be?

Young One, your family houses your history. For many years you were defined by your place within your family. Though the dynamic may not have been nurturing or safe, it was familiar. You began to perceive familiarity with your identity. As you grew, you had experiences that challenged that identity. You found your position within your family no longer held true for you as you saw yourself to be. Your family was not a part of that growth, and you felt the tension. You became acutely aware that the tension your familial role presented was in conflict with who you are. Your growth would insist that your family would also need to challenge their own roles and identities. Rather than risk the rift, you chose the familiar and played your role.

And if I choose to present as who I am, what of my family?

We have never been imbued with the power to choose for another. Your family could choose to set aside their expectations of you as they once knew you and see you as you are before them. There is also the risk of family not understanding who you have grown into being. With that risk, is the potential for abandonment and separation from your family unit.

I am shaken by the prospect of the latter. I know the reward of my freedom is not always won without loss. If I choose to accept the possibility of abandonment from my original family, how do I prepare?

You said, yourself, families come in many forms. In the end, the ones you choose will equally choose you. Prepare yourself by admitting loss is always a product of deconstruction, growth…life. The loss is necessary to create a space for the new.

I thank you, *Teacher*. I hear the wisdom of *Your* counsel and still feel the pain of choosing.

Dear *Teacher,*

I was conditioned to fear the natural world during my developmental, adolescent years. On a bright day, in a small rural area of DeRidder, I was enjoying the sun and gentle winds on my skin. I felt the freedom of the open air and of the fields of farmlands. My safety, then on that day, quickly turned into pain as I fought to loosen my leg from the bites of a Doberman much larger than my tiny body. As he stood atop me, I screamed. I do not recall if anyone came to my aid. I do remember, however, the loud and clear message of nature is not my friend.

Young One, humans are quite fragile beings with no talons, no wings, no camouflage and no shells to protect your physical vessels. Yes, pain is felt so much more viscerally, and your fear is palpable. All creatures of this Earth are vulnerable to another.

If that is true, it is no wonder we work so hard to destroy the natural world for our own preservation. What then is our incentive to protect the resources of this world when we are truly not safe?

You miss the larger perspective. All life has a universal law at play. That law is one of balance. If this is true, and also true is your fragility and vulnerability to the natural world, then what else must also be true given the law of balance?

It would seem paradoxical, but what must be true is that my life is dependent upon the natural world for my survival.

Yes, and that is the aspect of the law of balance.

My reacquainting with the natural world certainly was one of leaden progress. Each venture beyond the physical walls of my home and work was a stark reminder of the dangers that lay in wait ready to put out my tenuous life.

What prompted you to continue your ventures?

The noise and the human violence that surrounded me in my urban world held me in a state of constant, ill ease. I felt unsettled inside my *being*. I felt anxious and, dare I say, unsafe. I became aware of the natural world, though there were physical dangers, my fears and anxieties quieted. The more I ventured, the more okay I began to feel.

And what are your beliefs of the natural world today?

My beliefs are far distant from the time of my attack. Through my ventures, I discovered a safe space in my own *being*. Though there are real dangers and physical safety is not guaranteed, I can build and nurture in my *being*, safety. That safety is the unwavering knowing I am a part of the natural world. My relationship with the natural world and with the *law of balance* will build balance inside me and keep my fears checked. I can be free to once more revel in the sunlight and gentle winds upon my skin.

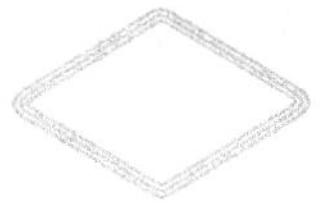

Dear *Teacher,*

What is the purpose of a teacher?

A teacher's purpose is several folds: to incite self-awareness to aspects of our true selves, to facilitate learning of the world around us and to bridge the two.

Foggy distant memories remind me of an experience I had with a teacher I held in high regard. Though the exact details escape me, the sharp feelings feel fresh in this moment. I recall sparring with a young person some ten years my junior. With each pulled punch and non-committed kick, I bested him. I believed I meant no true harm to him as I have always honored young ones with respect and regarded them as deserving of protection. Other students who were looking shared with our teacher I was assaulting one of our young ones. Though their intentions were playful, I internalized the chiding and felt ashamed. My teacher came to me and we began to spar. With every pulled-punch and non-committed kick, I was bested. I held my tears and hurried away. My grief charged the message received by my mind and insecurity; my teacher believed I intended harm. I learned how frail my image of being a protector was, and I was forced to question what was true. The truth was I intended no harm.

He taught you self-awareness.

I also learned idolizing teachers and heroes leave me vulnerable when my pedestal-elevating beliefs go unchecked. I am vulnerable to feelings of betrayal and hurt when those heroes, in their imperfections that anchor them, are unable to attain the heights unfairly laid upon them.

He taught you to question the world around you through your engagements with another being as an exemplar.

Another student asked about my reasons for leaving so abruptly. I communicated all I was experiencing in that moment including the feelings of distrust that I perceived to be real from our teacher. I do not remember the student's words as I drove away. My hurt and heart demanded of me a choice: return and accept my changed view of my teacher, or cling to my shattered image and discard all he had taught me.

The bridge.

Yes. That was the *bridge*. I chose to return with a more balanced view. I was to learn, much later, my teacher had not thought I would do harm to our young ones. He shared his hurt in causing me harm in that way. I unknowingly became the teacher, for him, in that moment.

And the lesson?

Teaching is a dynamic exchange between a teacher and a student, and the roles are fluid.

Dear *Teacher*,

I often have the belief and feeling I should be so much more than I am. I witness others in their lives, and I am reminded of the question that plagues my confidence…what am I doing with my life? Why does this question always come to me at my weakest?

Young One, notice your own awareness. The question arises in your weakest moments, those times and spaces where your hope and faith are thinned. I ask you, in what moments are those questions not permitted an audience with your consciousness?

I notice when I am being of true service do I feel aligned with that sacred *universal rhythm* and the questions quieted.

For example?

I was called to celebrate with a dear friend who, afflicted with degeneration of her muscles, was unable to move her own body as she had in her youth. Wanting to celebrate all she had shared with me in my learning and growth, I danced for her. As the music moved my body, I saw her moving in the ways she was able, though subtle. Her joyous smile and laughter radiated. My eyes watered as my gift was well received.

Were you enough, then, in that experience and in that moment?

I was enough as I remember that feeling. There was no need for me to be anyone or anything more than who I was.

And what were you in that moment and now?

I was a blessing given freely. Unknowingly, I often take my life for granted and disregard that my *being* has meaning and has purpose. I overlook how I am able to bring an expansive quality to other lives in, seemingly, the smallest of jesters: be it a smile, be it a laugh, or be it even the comfort of silence.

While all true, your being in the world also is wrought with responsibility. You may bring comfort to others in the smallest of ways; those ways can also bring great harm if wielded with disregard.

How do I know the difference?

Ask that part of you, your heart, which is bound by compassion to the collective human experience. Should there reside pain in that space, then harm has been caused. Should there be joy, then you have shared your own with another. Carry this responsibility with care. Know it does not ask of you to be any more than you are, but rather, it asks that you be a good steward of the blessing that is you.

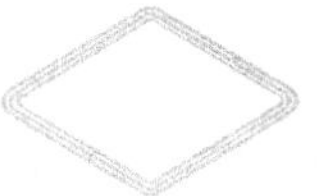

Dear *Teacher,*

We humans have a process known as *witnessing* or rather being fully present with another to share in his experience or her story. I had the honor of being witness to a young man's process. He was a year my junior during my time at the military academy. One unremarkable evening, he asked to see a cadet counselor and, with no context for the request, I accepted. We opened our conversation with seemingly, non-intrusive exchanges though his pain was obvious in his expression. I offered only my support free of judgment. Sensing sincerity, he shared he struggled with the tension of relinquishing his paternal rights to his unborn child and continuing his career at the military academy. He spoke, and I listened. He was silent, and I listened. He cried, and I listened.

You say you were listening. What was it that you were listening for?

I was listening for words, for inspiration that I might be able to share with him to help ease his pain. Instead, I became aware, I didn't have the words though a sacred, safe space of trust had been created. What was being shown before me was a different expression of what it meant to be masculine. His tearful expression was beyond the cultural norms, and my heart was filled with gladness for being able to be the *witness* he needed in that moment.

What happened next?

The words I searched for were spoken through inquiry. I asked him what meant the most to him and his life? In his heart, would he be able to be resolved about missing his child's birth, his child's first smile, his child's first steps or his child's first words? Would he be able to accept forgoing his career at the academy and not resent his family growing into being?

The moment we shared was based very much in all three. I could see his burden ease as he became more resolute in his choice. His breath eased. His tears subsided. His voice steadied. All about him was this air of calm and peace.

What blocked him was eliminated and his path forward became clear. By witnessing, you helped facilitate a process of discovery and healing for him in that moment.

What I also realized was that I have been a friend, confidant and counselor not only for him but also for others in my own life. I have, conversely, been the recipient of many such blessings from others as well. I had not fully realized the healing that comes via the very act of *witnessing* another. It is in those moments the burdens are shared, and the loads lightened, that we might step a little more confidently in the right direction.

Dear *Teacher,*

I am insecure by make-up, and I have never questioned my insecurities as teachers in their own rights. Too often have I succumbed to the judgments of others judging me as too dark, too skinny, common in intelligence.

Young One, your insecurities were met by those who feared being discovered as having similar insecurities.

With respect, that realization does little to ease the pain of those judgements. I began consuming the beliefs that I was not enough to be in the world whole and complete as I am; nor was I worthy of being loved. My internal world reflected how I believed myself to be in the outer world, invisible, and self-critical. Those who looked as I do never were given my attention as they were reminders of my own unresolved pain. And so, I chose to befriend "the lighter ones", "the stronger ones" and "the intelligent ones."

Did you find greater relief in those circles?

I found different insecurities surfaced.

And why would that be?

I sought validation in others rather than seeking my own.

Seeking others' approval for you and your life is fraught with pitfalls even by those who would hold your best interest at heart. Where did this discovery lead you?

I began to question what I approved of in my *being;* though, the list was far shorter than those defining what I abhorred. I questioned the imbalance. I questioned if I was replaying what others had said of me or were those truly my own voicings. Those that were my own, and those that elevated me, quieted when I asked them to do so. The voices that were not my own anchored and toyed with my pain. They offered no respite and heightened my insecurities with shattering, unceasing noise.

Young One, still you persisted. Your cries were heard. At your side, and all around, the light showed. It warmed you, inspired you and lit your way. The light in an act of self-kindness and in gentle self-thought, scattered the shadow voices long enough for you to feel the joy and support in the silence.

Thank you, *Teacher,* for your part. I hear new voices of support and self-affirmation in the *light.* My insecurities are still very present; though now, I have greater distinctions between those that warrant my attention and those that do not. I am aware of having greater capacities to accept and to love all parts of my *being* — to include my insecurities. In self-acceptance, my circle has grown welcoming those who look as I do. I am glad to make theirs and my acquaintances.

Young One, it has been some time that you and I have communed. Watching over this time, I see you have allowed yourself to grow distant, moving further from My guidance. Though you have free will, this is why I have called upon you to quiet, to settle, to realign with that which is natural.

Young One, it has been some time that you and I have communed. Watching over this time, I see you have allowed yourself to grow distant, moving further from My guidance. Though you have free will, this is why I have called upon you to quiet, to settle, to realign with that which is natural.

Dear *Teacher,* I have not felt my heart full for quite a while. Plainly, this is not a compelling reason for my absence but only an acknowledgement of the truth in *Your* words. For this, I am sorry.

None is needed. I call only to bring to your awareness the agitation and the uneasiness I feel by you falling out of your practices. These times you live in are filled with chaos and habits that give way to the lesser human instincts — addictions and sleeping sicknesses in all their forms. My calling is but a caution to stir your diligence and re-engagement with your disciplines.

I have not felt my discipline waver. I have regularly sat in silent meditation as I always do.

Yes, you have sat many times as you have always, but you have not crossed into the sacred space of quiet each time.

I do not understand.

How often have you felt the silence in your meditations? How often have you allowed your thoughts, or your emotions, to order and to control that time of your meditation? How often have you completed your time with no greater clarity or ease than before you began?

I feel the distinction. I have sat but rarely, as of late, in meditation. I have allowed myself to be steered by routine. It has been in my routine where I have allowed a break in my devotion and discipline. I am reminded that my meditation time is charged by what is in my heart and not by my mundane, mental images. How do I be more present, more resolute, when my mind is stronger than my heart's intentions?

You speak the truth of your moment. You ask for the help of Divine support to bring quiet to your mind. Justly, allow the mind to simply be. To tangle with the mind only brings greater noise.

Dear *Teacher*, I call upon *Your* support. I have struggled with my mental entrapments as they have darkened my clarity. I have struggled with my emotions as they have held me paralyzed in my disingenuous routines. I am in need of *Your* blessing so that I might return to the *quiet*, to the silence and receptive to divine inspiration.

And so it is. I give you My blessing. Be still and be comforted.

Dear *Teacher*,

I come to you in hopes that my heart will be eased, and my grief soothed. I am hurting with the death of my remaining grandparent. Though my adult life was spotted with few moments of time with her, I question the indefensible reasons for not being more intentional in deepening my relationship with her. So much came into focus during the celebration of her life. Many remembered her fondly and yet others fought over her favor. Why does death unleash the ugliness of we humans?

Young One, Death is but a natural course in the cycle of all life. Humans are the only creatures fighting to avoid Death's calling at all costs. Death like all things has its sacred purpose – to till the spaces for renewal and new beginnings. Humans grab, cling and refuse to accept the universal truth – all things die. When we are faced with the inconvenience of Death, we are made consciously aware of all the unrealized potential, the unspoken words, the unmanifested desires and the unresolved of lost moments.

Is it not possible that Death also reveals the blessings of a life well lived?

No one side is absolute. Death offers many gifts. It is the responsibility of those in the throws of Death's presence to make alliance or foe with Death. It is through that choice that Death will reveal its blessings or crippling hold.

Your wisdom resonates. Those who could not accept her death, allowed their own grief to consume them. Their actions and words reflected their pain. Those who remembered her fondly through their grief, shared many instances of her lifetime of service. She nurtured her eight children; she consoled her community; she fashioned quilts to warm those in need. I saw, in those moments, the gift of service passed from her to my own mother and so on to me. My own habit of service was born of generations who embraced community and their desire to bring into being a better humankind than what we inherited.

We each receive gifts from our ancestors. Not all are clear and not all are comfortable to bear. We may be gifted artisans; we may be exciters to action; we may be workers of the land. And still, we may be simply steady in our way of being. It is through Death that we are awakened to our unresolved and our love for those lost.

And how might I discover my other gifts if not solely through the loss of loved ones?

I ask you, what comes seemingly effortless to you that may be challenging to others? What has been admired about your way of being? How do you experience the world around you? Do you see, hear, feel what others do not, yet you know is real? Your discovery begins with an acceptance and acknowledgement of the lineage that brought you into being. There, you will discover your gifts.

So it is. I give thanks to those who have come before me. May I do you honor in my service and in my guardianship of the gifts bestowed upon me. Through my deeds, may you live on.

Dear *Teacher,*

I acknowledge I've had embarrassment and shame regarding how I have engaged other humans. Too often I bedded many with the belief I was seeking a real relationship. I succumbed to the notion I was not worthy of another's attention if I were not parading my body in ways intended to stir heat.

What were your true intentions?

I sought validation; I sought affection; I sought intimacy in its truest sense — to know and to *see* another and to be known and to be *seen.*

And your rendezvous were not uncommon. Humans, by nature, are social creatures. That desire to be in community, in relationship, often gets blurred in how to manifest that need. What were the outcomes in how you chose to sexually express your desire for a relationship?

I was left feeling far removed from validation, community and intimacy. I experienced shame, depletion in my sense of wellbeing and emotional fragility.

You come to me now with this knowledge. Along the way you had an awareness of the need for change, yes?

I did. I let go and surrendered to my own process. For many years afterward, I set aside my carnal desires. I questioned, with intention, what I needed. I discovered the intimacy I sought was one with my own *being.* I desired to reacquaint me with *me.* I desired to remember that place of self-love before I took on the cultural beliefs I had to look and be in ways counter to my nature.

Young One, as I am hearing you, you discovered your own validation?

It was more than validation. I found a place of forgiveness. I found a way to welcome my experiences; to learn from them; and to be grateful for a time in my life that served to heal and to strengthen my self-awareness. Ultimately, there was a strengthening of my character.

What does your newfound knowledge do for your desire to be in relationship with others?

I have greater clarity. I can separate my carnal desire and not from a place of disavowing that part of my being. But rather, I can do so in a way that supports my clarity of intention. I am able to assess if there is an invitation for intimacy, growth and mutual beneficial exchanges beyond lying with another. I can ask will we both be better for having known one another. If yes, I can allow myself to continue in exploration. If, on the other hand, the answer is no, I can be on my separate way with confident resolve.

Then you have learned the lesson. May it serve you well.

Dear *Teacher*,

I had the wonderful opportunity to travel once more. During my time abroad, I experienced a surprising sadness, a longing, for home. This home was not the physical place from where I traveled, but rather, it was for the place I found myself in at the time. I was struck by a sense of grief based in the potential of leaving the old for the new.

Young One, it is natural to wrestle between the desire for the new, the exciting, and the comforts of the familiar. The difficulty for most is distinguishing if the call for change is real or an avoidance of lesson-bearing circumstances. If the first is true, there is an alignment that flows in support of one opportunity opening to subsequent ones. However, if avoidance is the motivation, then opportunities for change will stagnate. The circumstances of grappling with unlearned lessons will be the reality with simply different surroundings and different characters.

How, then, do I know the difference?

Sit in the silence. Reflect on your motivations. Does the message you receive have weight? Does it have a foundation in reality or fantasy? Is the message you receive consistent or does it ebb and flow without solid foundation? Are your mind, body, emotions, and spirit in agreement, and do they energize action needed for change. Is that energized action sustainable with no guarantees of outcomes? Do you feel a deeper knowing of the rightness of change? And, are their signposts manifesting to validate right-action towards change? These are the questions to consider.

But, there are times when change has happened without my wishing it so. What then?

The process is still unchanged. Whether we actively choose to initiate change or it is chosen for us, we must sit in the silence. By opening to the pain, to the loss, to the anger, and to whatever combinations thereof, we empower a releasing and a rebuilding on all levels.

In any moment, then, I can feel loss.

Yes. The loss of what could have been can be experienced as deeply as what was or what is.

Why, then, should I participate in my life if loss can be felt in every moment of change and possibility?

In each of them, there also exists the possibility to experience joy and wonder. The depths of your ability to feel loss are equal to your ability to feel love.

Deeply hurting, deeply loving, releasing, rebuilding. With focus — embrace the change. So is my lesson. Thank you, my *Teacher.*

Dear *Teacher*,

I have had another hiatus. The start and stops of my convictions have grown more frequent. I find my focused attention shorter. My calm is less so. I have the experience of dis-ease creeping in moment by moment.

Younger One, you are chasing an illusion. I hear you pleading for greater affluence, for the perfect partner, to be the best healer, to be the best artist, to have this or that. Each is but a distraction and holds you in the place of belief you are not enough.

But I have such a desire to be better than enough. I feel I have potential to grow and to learn.

You confuse curiosity, inspiration and the manifestation of one's potential with deviating from your nature. Deviating is for the purpose of satisfying other's expectations for who and what you ought to be. Would you be satisfied with a human sharing their life with you while also accepting your faults?

…Yes.

Would you accept them if they were of another race, another religion, less than able bodied, older or younger than you, less pretty than how you define beauty?

I would have to say no. I have expectations of who and what they should be.

This is the point. In all areas of your life, you open yourself to afflictions of longing. You step further and further from your essential nature to chase fantastical ideas of what the perfect life would be for you.

I am hearing I should simply accept my circumstances without pursuit.

Then you are not listening. Pursuit for the purpose of filling a void is perpetually non-filling. Pursuit for the purpose of manifesting your greatest potential, in alignment with your true nature, fills your cup abundantly. In that space, you are wanton for nothing more than to be.

How do I distinguish the difference?

Ask, does the pursuit bring you joy. Is there consistency in your effort? Do you experience each of your parts in alignment? If each answer is yes and true, then you are following your true nature and are receptive to the universal blessing of support. If no, on the other hand, then prepare yourself to continue in your longing.

I have much work to do so that I may stand in the certainty of my nature and so that I may have the courage to withstand the forces telling me the contrary. *And so, it is.*

Dear *Teacher,*

It amazes me how there can be moments of clarity even in the noise of every-day life. Piercing my consciousness was an awareness of how we humans wear many masks: masks to keep others at a distance; masks to seduce; masks to conform; masks to blend unnoticed; masks to disrupt.

Young One, we have discussed all things have their purpose. What are those masks?

They have helped me survive and cope in a society of norms. Though at each place of my life, the masks shifted and informed me that my old ways of sur-vival were insufficient. They grated against my true self.

Were the masks always there for you?

No. As far back as I can recall, I put on my first when I got the message I did not belong. My skin was too dark to be acceptable.

But your skin is unchangeable. So, what was the mask you created?

It was one of intelligence. If I were smart enough, I would belong. I found that was not to be true, however. Others would not allow even a moment to wel-come me. The intelligence mask failed me.

Which then came into being?

Humor and charm did. I wielded them through my smile, the glint in my eye and the softening of my posture. I was welcomed into circles previously closed to me. To others, I was presumed soft, without character and unworthy of being known. I felt another departure from my true self still. I began to realize

I was not able to be what others expected or chose for me to be. The masks hurt too much. Buckling under their weight, I fell, dropping into the centers of emptiness, grief and depression.

You have learned in order to be accepted by other humans is always conditional and predicated on, above all things, theirs and your personal comforts.

I feel I am not yet ready to discard my masks but rather deploy them in a conscious way while not accepting them as my true self. Doing so, I can release the tethers of human expectations. Even in this awareness, I feel a sense of freedom.

There is freedom, yes. There is also a caution, Young One. I caution you to be diligent in the endeavor to view your masks with objectivity. For the entrapments of unchallenged masks are ever present.

Dear *Teacher,*

It has been said the orbits of our friendships and relations are mirrors for who we have chosen to be at periods in our lives. Then at pivots, seeds of disruption touch those orbits causing fissures in the grounds upon which we have built our identities. The result is chaos.

Young One, those orbits exist as reflections of our values and what our hearts hold as truth in those periods. The seeds that are introduced are attractions of different focuses. They are different desires for ways of being that some part of us has willed into the substantive reality of our changing orbit.

Why, then, is chaos the outcropping of this process?

The seeds' purposes are to awaken us and to force our awareness to patterns that no longer define who and what we are growing into being. The seeds take root. They begin to unravel the internal and the external around us all the conditions counter to the new.

What if I am not ready for the change because it is too painful? How do I stop the process? How do I pluck the sprouted seeds at their roots?

Once introduced, and the taproot placed, the process cannot be undone. We may ignore or slow the unfolding, but the new will come to blossom. Though not always comfortable, navigating the change may be done through surrender and acceptance. These forces, like the seeds, are attractive and bring with them the influences that water and nurture the new. The growth and maturation of those sprouted seeds transform our orbits to reflect outwardly what has manifested internally.

Does this phenomenon explain the comings and goings of friendships and relationships in all their forms?

This is exactly the phenomenon. The pain and discomfort arise when we have attached our identities to that which we have surrounded ourselves with. We believe we are the athlete, the skinny girl, the brain, the father, the recluse. When we recognize we are all those and have the capacity to go beyond those limiting identities, do we open to a greater expression of who we are and allow a greater fluidity to those orbits surrounding us. From that place, our response to the chaos of change becomes tampered.

How do I recognize when I am in that process?

Take note of who and what is coming and going into your orbit along with the velocity of that change. Then ask, "Am I holding onto that which is no longer working in my life?" Ask, "Am I ready for surrender for the sake of greater possibilities?" Should the answers be yes, then the process has begun.

Dear *Teacher*,

I am uneasy. Each moment that I felt I had progressed in finding balance, I teetered into darkness. My addictions, in their gross and subtle forms, drove my habits that would counterbalance those addictions into dysfunction. My addictions to exercise, to work, to digital interfaces of computers and cell phones covered me in distraction. My attention shifted from personal awareness regarding my safety, nurturance and health.

Young One, human addictions are dangerous to your well-being when unchecked. Addictions are energetic vortices within you and are fueled by external catalysts. They are perpetual cycles laying waste in their wakes.

You have said, though, all things have their lessons.

That is true of addictions as well. On the ends of their expressions, they illuminate places where you are unresolved. In order to realize the lesson, however, you must survive the experience. Addictions are self-serving, always, at the expense of your well-being.

I want to survive. I want to fulfill my purpose for this life. And, my forms of addictions are not always apparent.

Each addiction has a mechanism designed to reward the user. Do not confuse reward with feeling good. Rewards come in many disguises from distraction, to dissociation from your circumstances, to euphoria, to joy and to the gamut of all of the in-betweens. The reward has an immediacy in its results from the start. The addiction, itself, provides signposts when seeking the reward. The first are your thoughts. Do they remind you of the engagement in the addiction or project the future promise of the desired reward? The second is locked in the body's memory. Was there euphoria signaled by the high? The third are the emotions. Do you experience fear or even anger with cessation and non-reward? Do you experience joy when the reward manifests and grief when it ends? The last is about the cycle frequency and the duration of engagement in the addictions. The more frequent the engagement is the more destructive the addiction becomes.

Knowing the mechanisms does not help me to understand how to stop my addictions.

There is not one channel suited for all variations and nuances of addictions. Each can be disrupted to shift their cycle in the direction of balance. Ultimately, the cycle disruptions begin with choice. Choose to see them without pretense, without delusion. Choose to seek and receive support. Choose a different way.

Dear *Teacher,* I do not know if I am prepared enough or courageous enough to choose.

You may choose to not choose through your inaction. In that place of paralysis, your addictions will always be there holding you captive to your lower, baser self and… you are so much more.

Dear *Teacher,*

My eyes have often deceived me while projecting what I believe to be true. Many faulty judgments have been the result. I do not know the countless opportunities I have missed out of my believing and acting, without interrogating what my eyes have shown me.

Young One, humans perceive their world through many senses. The eyes are but one. How often have you looked on a situation and drawn the conclusion of the situation only to find it to be quite different when questioned?

Why do I have sight if it cannot present absolute truth?

There are many levels to experiencing what is real. Humans have but a very limited capacity to perceive the All. Each sense offers but a glimpse. The All is greater than you or I. Each of us is but a fraction, of a fraction, of that Expression. Human laziness, at its root, is quick to judge. True understanding is engendered by patient observation with the totality of one's being. Understanding is not informed by absolutes but rather relativity.

What I feel from *Your* guidance is conflict. *You* have stated to know truth is to perceive with all of my being and yet *truth* is relative.

Therein lie our limitations. Up can only be, relative to down, in one instance. The same up can, however, be down when perceived through a different sense or point of observation.

If so, I would have to conclude the need to apply *Your* guidance to human engagement as well. I have known so many and, in retrospect, have not really known them. I have made judgments of their being, and of their character, while assuming I knew the sum of their circumstances from a single engagement. I am realizing my laziness, but curiously, I also notice my fear. If I ask more deeply and provide allowances for another to show up as he or she chooses, I would create a space of vulnerability for him or her to ask about me. And I fear what he or she would find in me.

The difficult truth is we can never know the totality of another's being. To presume so is of the highest arrogance. To inquire, with sincerity, is to express compassion. Do not be deluded in the belief you will be loved and adored by all with whom your path may cross. But if you can open your heart and seek to understand, you may find your fear quieted.

I feel a wave of peace cresting, dampening my resistance. I feel closer to whole with this new awareness and must also laugh at knowing that I must, equally, regard myself with relativity. Through self-inquiry, I can be in self-compassion. Thank you, once more, my *Teacher*.

Dear *Teacher,*

I feel we are on the tipping point of great change. Human emotion runs rampant. In every corner, we are engaged in distraction clinging to the impermanent possessions we've deluded ourselves in believing are real. The more we obtain, the greater the fears of loss and destitution.

Young One, you have learned to listen with your being, to the subtle rhythms of the natural order. Not only are humans participating in but are actively facilitating a shift in collective consciousness. No longer sufficient is the great-sleep cocoons humans have sheltered themselves within. All of what you have believed to be true is unraveling.

The imagery of instability sits restless within my body, mind and emotions. I sense the erratic behaviors and the unpredictability of we humans.

Then settle into the Silence. It is always there, always present.

I can breathe, and I feel centered. How do I be in the space of *stillness* when I sense so much suffering even in those who are not consciously aware of their own pain?

You too were not aware in your youth, in your sleep. Only when you began to inquire about your true nature did you come to realize your pain; to recognize your pain; to feel your pain; and to ally with your pain. Being in stillness calms the torrents within. Others will feel the stillness in your presence, and for a moment, they will experience quiet. They will want to stay but cannot. When returned to their own circumstances, they will once more feel the unrest and conflict. Yet they will have received the experience of another way of being. So be still in your example, unmoved in your resolve. Know we each have the right to learn in our own way, even if through our pain.

Your guidance indicates through being in stillness, we each have the opportunity for reprieve. More than that, I can recognize human pain is an unerring learning ground inherent in the human condition. Pain brings growth if I have the courage to allow it. But, surely no human wants to suffer.

Yet, you constantly engage in circumstances that ripen the conditions for suffering. You surround yourself with others who are prone to addiction as you are. And you engage be it to sex, to drugs, to avoidance or to distraction. You tell half-truths; feed on nutritionally, impoverished foods; participate in activities for the high. When the effects of choices and chance align, you ask "Why me?"

Only until we learn to listen, and equally important, to follow the *natural order* can we lessen our pain and step more fully into grace and gratitude? I, too, will need reminding of *Your* counsel. My own humanness would have me welcome sleep and ignorance; and I also am aware that what is real is not bound by the human whims of want.

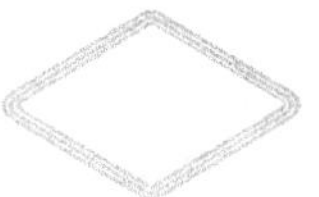

Dear *Teacher,*

I have felt in a place of non-belonging for so long. My family I was born into was webbed with chaos, and I was the part out of sync. There were countless moments I was unable to understand why I felt so misplaced. As I matured, I distanced and convinced myself that my family would never understand or accept who I knew myself to be. Along the way, many others entered and left my life. Through it all, I desired to feel a sense of home. Those who came into my life shared the difficulties they experienced with forming relations with me. They shared with me their wanting to be a part of my life and my ego, my pride, would not accept their characterizations of me. I held to the perspective they could only be a part of my life if they conformed to my liking and comfort. *Young One, you are not alone. Histories and scores of your ancestors have held the notion the cycles of universal rhythms are bound to your wills. Never has it been, nor will it ever be so. It is true we each have our divine script as co-creators of our circles of experiences. Out of those comes our teaching. What were you shown in your circles?* I was shown a cloistered life. Few traveled with me and my loneliness deepened. Sheltering in the privacy of my own spaces showed me a deep darkness where little joy resided. I felt pain and I was left with the question, "Why am I alone?"

We heard your call. Only you could choose to listen for the light of guidance and support that was always there for you.

In those times of silence, I was forced to reconcile the distance between what I knew was possible in my life and what was manifesting. I began to see the walls I built around my inner young one; the barriers I created around my heart; and the cages I formed around my love.

What purpose did they serve?

They kept me from experiencing. They kept me safe. They held me bound in place while never venturing out of my self-imposed solitude. And, I was the source of my pain. I saw, clearly, my oath to self-imprisonment. As I removed one brick, two bricks and yet another to my barriers, my pain lessened. I became aware of the many missed opportunities to share with others the genuine connections that were presented to me. The more barriers I dismantled, the more joy I began to experience. My heart warmed. I found a key; and the caged love I carried was freed.

What all does this have to do with your family?

There were those who traveled with me from the start. They waited patiently to be welcomed. When I was ready, they were there. In their words and deeds, they validated what I had built within. They reflected back to me that I had found home in them through finding home within my own being. I am grateful to them and to those who came before them. My *Teacher*, I learned I have many teachers; and for that I give thanks, for I am home.

Dear *Teacher*,

My sleep was very active last evening. My dreamtime was filled with a violence I have not known in some time. Though violent, I experienced no fear, no regret, no anger. There was but a sense of rest and of calm. I am unable to make sense of my experience.

Young One, dreams are portals humans use in all manners to bring order and sense to their lives. Dreams bring to awareness the unresolved, what is and what is to come. They also can be a bridge to what inspires and to what heals.

I do not understand. The dream, it seems, does not fit into any of the fields *You* have shared with me as I sit with this dream and its meaning. Dare I say the dream, itself, does not feel like my own. Its imagery, its violence feels foreign to my own nature and who I sense myself to be. How is that so?

Humans are social creatures. There are many facets to what makes you as individuals and collectively. The collective, shared experiences are often believed to affect all others and not just you as the individual. Therein lies your blind spot. Humans are sensitive and experience the emotions of others even if not consciously aware. True, there are those among you who feel to a greater degree the pains and joys of others. Nonetheless, there are the gross and subtle exchanges you experience in your interactions. Each emotion carries with it imagery.

As I hear you, am I to understand that the dream I experienced may very well not be my own but another's? Thinking on my experiences, I do remember instances where my emotional state moved to align with a friend's, a family member's and even a stranger's. I have innumerable experiences of feeling joyful in one moment and quite agitated in the next after crossing paths with someone in a space of negativity. I do not understand how this translates to my dreams though.

Let me ask you, if you can feel another's emotion and emotion carries imagery, what can you suppose about the effects on your dreams?

The imagery coupled with emotional charge creeps into my unconscious, and I play out the situation in my dreamtime. When I am unaware that I have assumed another's emotions, my dreams do their part to bring resolution and to release the aspects that are not my own.

Precisely.

If I suppose correctly, how do I first become aware when I am holding another's emotions and more importantly, how do I release them?

The process begins with empathy and the recognition we each have our process. We are each responsible for our own growth. With that knowledge, we open up to choosing to carry another's process or not. There are many ways of letting go. This is but one.

Dear *Teacher,*

Accountability causes me discomfort. For reasons beyond my conscious memories, I have feared making mistakes. Mistakes have engineered my beliefs of how I may be perceived. I cannot be seen or known as less than competent. I cannot be imperfect. For these reasons, I have shied from accountability and from taking risks in my growth. My fragile ego weakens under the weight of accountability.

Young One, accountability too often is held in the notion that there must be necessary loss: loss of privacy, loss of one's ideas of self, loss of anonymity. Accountability holds so much more when embraced. It holds the gift of integrity; it embraces one's personal power; it fosters an intimate knowing and an appreciation for the precious gift of life. As we embrace accountability, we then hold ourselves responsible for making our lives worth living.

How might I embrace accountability when I never care to be at the center of attention?

Accountability has many aspects. In and of itself, accountability is dynamic. Only through action does accountability live and breathe. The question begins with who or what are you accountable to.

I am often accountable to *You.* I am accountable to my family, to my friends, to my co-workers and to those whom I serve.

Why are you accountable to all those you have named?

They depend on me to show up and be as they would have me be. When I am anything other than they perceive, there is disappointment, which I feel deeply.

I am accountable to them because I have chosen to be so. They are representations of different pillars in my life. Without them, my foundation is unsteady.

They are pillars, yes; but your foundation is not rooted in them. You have overlooked a critical player to whom you are accountable. Who might that be?

Me.

Without holding yourself accountable to your own commitments to being who and what you are and what you can be, you will always be flappable under the wills and wishes of others. Self-accountability strengthens your sense of self and empowers you with the courage to venture where you may not have otherwise.

I feel the gravity of this truth. It is far easier for me to hold myself accountable to others because I am invested in being respected and kept in their good graces. Yet, I do not hold myself accountable to me. I have my practice backwards. Out of self-accountability blossoms a consistency of being that bears the fruit of respect of others and enables a life well lived. I understand and will effort to be accountable to my word, to my deed and to me.

Dear *Teacher,*

I have been sitting with the idea of *resolution*. I have carried so much baggage with me throughout my life. Not wanting to truly rummage through the pains and disappointments, the loads grew to backbreaking weights. Each day was numb to joyful experiences. Relationships fractured in my internal and external worlds. The reflection I saw staring back was filled with shame. In the quiet moments, memories crept from my subconscious whispering messages of times, places and spaces that were left incomplete. Frozen are those people and events as they were when I knew them, and most assuredly, I am for them when they knew me.

Young One, each moment is discrete. Too often that is forgotten, and humans would like to change the moment to their liking. If it felt intoxicating in all measures and senses, humans want to hold on. If it was painful, they want to bury the moment and discard it. Each time there is that memorable engagement with a moment or experience, there is a resonance begging for resolution.

I clearly feel *resolution* is more than an idea. There are experiences that I still feel in my body and see in my thoughts though they are many years removed from the present.

It is that very dynamic that keeps the experience alive in your present. It is the emotion experienced at that moment that fills you with the backbreaking baggage. The unconscious and the body remember; though, the conscious mind may not. They remember what is unresolved.

My human tendency is to attribute experiences with being positive or negative as a result of how I felt in the moment. I would further qualify them as life giving or destructive even if on the subtlest of levels. When I further question the feeling of resolution, I notice an equal tendency of tagging negative experiences as the ones needing resolve.

Resolution does not care how humans have experienced a moment. Resolution is a cycle; it is a process. Resolution demands completion of the moment that had an initiation, a journey and a conclusion. It is in the journey, where the cycle of resolution may stall. Humans hold on or they run while not allowing the cycle to come to its natural conclusion. For positive experiences, giving thanks for the moment while acknowledging it as whole and complete is to be resolved. For the negative experiences, processing the emotion, allowing it to pass from your body and building an alliance with the memory to nurture in you wisdom, is to be resolved.

Mentally, it appears far easier to resolve positive, emotional experiences over negative ones. My body speaks through its own wisdom countering and sharing with me positive experiences can equally anchor me to what was. They can keep me from truly being in the present and fearful of future risks of positive or negative outcomes.

Resolution, as a practice, is not an easy one, but it will provide for you greater capacity to live and be in your life now. Little time will be spent in what was or what could be.

Dear *Teacher,*

Human relationships are curious things in that there are so many different fashions and types. Our thoughts and emotions are swayed from the everyday, casual conversations with unknowns to the depthless communications with intimates. Each relationship, I have noticed, has a cycle. Some persevere through many days, months and years. Others are done in a single breath. My desire for connection is ever present if only in the backgrounds of my unconscious. With that said, I am not always aware of the reasons I entered into a relationship.

Young One, conscious awareness is not static; but rather, conscious awareness demands the intentional actions of interrogating our motivations. The very acknowledgement of being aware you are not aware opens a space to choose. When we begin relating to another, having an understanding of our motives enables us to judge the value of the relationship.

If I understand *You,* I will be able to better understand my needs and contributions to the relationship as an outcome of knowing my starting place in the relationship. There feels to be many implications to not having this awareness. One potential might be the abdication of my right to have a voice in the relationship.

How might that abdication manifest?

From the outset, I might not share my wishes and desires for the sake of maintaining normalcy and surface comfort in the relationship. I might subjugate my need for emotional support and understanding to the needs of others. I might lock myself away, secluded and distant from the emotional reaches of others. My relationships have rarely withstood these disengagements be they my own or that of the other.

You spoke to all relationships having a cycle, which is true. Your reflection began with the opening to the relationship, and you have now alluded to the ending of relationships. That too is a conscious or an unconscious action with differing outcomes. Why would that be?

If the relationship was entered into consciously and served its purpose, it may close with the completeness of a shared experience. Conversely, if the relationship ended without resolution, I sense constant wondering. I sense anger and resentment arresting my creative engagements in my life. The bound energy feeds my judgment of self-worth, and I am left with the question of what was so flawed in me and in my character that crashed the relationship. I cling to what was, to what should have been and to the desire for validation.

And so it goes, all cycles of relationships have a beginning, a maturing, and an ending. How you engage with the end is the start of a new cycle. That may be a start of a cycle of regret or one of forgiveness and joy for having exchanged with another in a mutually beneficial way. Choose consciously. Choose wisely.

Dear *Teacher,*

While sitting with my thoughts, I was reminded of a long-ago friend. He was afflicted with a treatable form of pancreatic cancer, and he was overcoming all odds for survival. At the time, I agreed to be present for him and his family should he pass. We fell out of communication, though, for a lack of effort on both our parts. I realized I carried *guilt.* Why is that if he and I both were equally to blame for the dissolution of our friendship?

Young One, human guilt is a complex emotion and pattern. Guilt manifests as an outcome of agreements, and of promises, we make be they unconscious or conscious. At the root of guilt, is the agreement to serve others before self. Though service, in and of itself, can be creative and healing, wielding the expectations of service for power and control can be quite destructive.

Does this necessarily mean *guilt* is destructive?

When I speak of destruction, I mean that which is antithetical to life. Destruction can and does occur on many levels from the macro of natural disasters to the physical, cellular level. Guilt acts at the cellular level, as in the case of your friend's cancer, by constricting the flows of your natural rhythms. Guilt activates your stressors.

Physiologically, this makes sense and is all too simplistic a definition of *guilt* and its mechanisms. How do the emotional components contribute to the complexity of *guilt?*

At the root is the desire to be of service. We give our word to doing what we are able in order to fulfill that commitment. Wrapped in that promise is compassion. When our word is broken, be it perceived or real, the compassion trigger is activated bringing to our awareness we are in some way out of integrity. We are out of integrity in our relationship to our promise or we are out of integrity with our own truth.

When I experience *guilt*, I notice there is a sense of blame. I have been both the recipient of blame from others and have also inflicted self-blame.

Blame is the sustenance, the food, which enables guilt to grow while never being satiated.

How do I end the cycle of *guilt* then?

The process begins with an understanding of the agreement you have made. Does it still serve a beneficial purpose given current circumstances? Does the agreement need altering, or does it need dissolution altogether? The awareness you have regarding the motivation of your agreements will enable you to disempower the pattern of guilt. That may only be done through understanding your nature, your needs and your capacity to be of service.

Dear *Teacher*,

There is a decaying of courtesy in our lives. That is the art of listening, not listening for the sake of just hearing, but listening to understand. These days are ones of impatience and intolerance. Man, woman, and child are treating one another with levels of disregard that devalue each other's humanness. Our tempers are ignited by half-truths, incomplete stories and an arrested development of our emotional intelligence. I am also guilty of engaging in assumptions and, subsequently, moved to action by clips of half-truths.

Young One, it is no coincidence human behavior has devolved into a dynamic of violence and chaos as an outcome of intolerance. Human history is fraught with many examples. The illusions and delusions at play are designed to distract from the true work of understanding your being within the context to the greater Whole.

How is understanding my deeper, true nature a precursor to me listening to understand another?

As you grow in your capacity of self-knowing, you are presented with numerous gifts, talents and frailties that make you, you. Each aspect, when viewed through different lenses, informs how you see others. Not only will you be able to discern with greater precision your motivations, but you will also be more capable of unearthing external influences.

Following your wisdom, then, indicates my self-awareness is my locus of strength. By extension, self-awareness engenders greater confidence to explore, with sincerity, that which I perceive as other. *You* have named distractions on a number of occasions, beyond our current context, as culprits that interfere with self-awareness. I can't help but feel time, as we engage with it, as a distraction. The pace of everyday life necessitates a quickness that impacts my attention and my ability to listen to others intently.

Time is an excuse humans use to absolve themselves of responsibility. Humans reference time as being in short supply and in high demand. Time is something that is done to you rather than you allying with the time you have to focus your attention. If you listen to understand, there is a degree of work that is necessary. "I do not have time to listen" is a convenience that provides an escape.

I feel deflated as well as the need to confess, at times, I don't care to understand and would rather go about my life without engaging with another.

There is the truth. It is not about time. It is not about a lack of capacity or even a lack of ability, but rather will.

Where I will my attention is where I empower and energize my capacity to listen, to understand. By starting with self-awareness, I can ask if I have enough investment to sit with another, to inquire, to learn and to see myself in them. I understand. With much gratitude, thank *You.*

Dear *Teacher,*

I woke with a heavy heart. Tears are at their fullest, and I am saddened. My grief is housed in accepting that I will not ever be seen as anything more than a danger because of my brown skin. I am an unknowable danger in the places I live to those who benefit from the constructs of our inequitable culture. My skin tone agitates and stirs so much fear and anger in them. Concern for my own safety shuts up my reaching for relationships with others.

Young One, all beings have equal rights to be, to live, to love and to be loved. Power, and its application, has been perverted out of the base roots of human fear. The color of your skin is front and center reflecting back a different way of being and a different expression of the Divine Blessing of life.

If it were true that I have an equal right to live my life, history would have me question this. The violence against people of color would have me believe there is divine sanction for positions of authority and power. Scales of balance tip to favor and to preserve inequities. They serve as chains to my being in connection with others.

Your perception is informed by a single aspect of long histories of human cycles. Humans began their journey through the instinct of survival, and along the way, subjugated other humans to ensure that survival. Round and round humans have gone exchanging positions of dominance. Races have been both victims and aggressors. The difference is in scale only.

I can't accept that because, if I were to, I would also have to accept my invalid aspirations and feeble attempts to affect change. I would have to embrace the belief that the structures in place are a correction for past atrocities.

Logically that would make sense. Consider, however, what it would mean to lay down the scales of winner versus loser, to step out of the current cycle of desire for complete domination, and to create a new cycle based in accountable action to one's own integrity. Consider investigating your own fear instead of placing the fault in others. Consider inquiring about your own choices for how you present yourself in your life, be it from the perspective of gratitude and service, or from the perspective of despair and cynicism. Consider your desire to connect, and your lack of action, is but a function of your choice and not of the circumstances to which you are born.

I am struggling with the idea that my life, regardless of circumstance, still requires my active choosing of how to be in my life. However, when I feel into the vibration of *Your* message, there is an alignment. I feel even in the most horrific of times and spaces, I can choose to carry anger and bitterness. I can equally choose to open to a grace and a freedom that enables me to connect with all that is, including other humans.

I see you and my council is not without compassion. My gift to you is inspiration. May my words motivate you to actively be in your life and to receive the rapture of a life well lived.

Dear *Teacher*,

I am often amazed by my ability for delusion. There was a time I believed myself to be kind. I believed I would not do harm to another. I believed my intentions were plain despite their misalignment with my actions. Kindness was equated with a smile masking my true intention.

Young One, the web of the human complex is complicated by the mental circuses created for the purpose of preserving false beliefs. The false belief that you are your mind, and who you perceive yourself to be, is based in your deep sleep. The sleep is one so profound that it, in and of itself, would have you fight to protect against your awakening.

Are *You* saying, then, my delusions are the *sleep*?

I am saying your delusions are but a symptom.

How am I to know if I am asleep?

You, yourself, alluded to the key when you shared your smile would run counter to your conviction. Your mind would have you believe they are one in the same. Your emotions would signal discord. Your body would experience an elevation of stress, subtle or acute as it might be.

I enacted cruelty on many occasions under the guise of being kind. I would not speak my heart because I did not want to cause pain. Unknowingly, I would cause a different kind of hurt as I hurt. I withheld affection sourced in the twisted belief that I did not want to be perceived as fragile and impotent. I used my humor to maim while feeling the target's pain as my own. When I reflect, there was discord. My mind propelled me to action while my body suffered a bleed of anxiety.

There is an implication here that bears mention. Kindness is not always rooted in feeling good. The great sleep necessitates a deficit in awareness of intention amplified by unconscious action. You are asleep when you believe you are acting out of kindness while unconsciously causing hurt. Contrarily, you are awake when you intend towards speaking your truth from a foundation of care for self and other. Truth, though not always comfortable, delivers kindness as a byproduct. It is the type of kindness that enables the awakening to what is.

This seed of wisdom twirls around while the *great sleep* desperately flails to rot that seed at its roots. That seed would have me question my intention, question my action, and by extension, question my delusion. I am aware of my responsibility to listen when internal discord arises. I am aware of the potent harm that could result from my unwillingness to listen, from my unwillingness to question and to act in accordance with my truth.

And the responsibility to your truth is yours and yours alone. Do with it what you will and know that whatever the choice, there is always a reconciling. And so, it is.

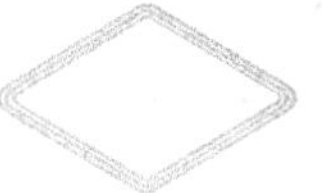

Dear *Teacher,*

I feel so much noise around. Death, destruction and violence are voluminous. So much so, it is difficult to find the counterbalances of love, forgiveness and inspiration. It is increasingly more difficult for me not to give in to my complacency and yield to the notion that what I do makes no difference.

Young One, every action makes an impact. What you are experiencing is friction from your own discomfort. The friction is your grief and anger rawly confronting your desire for stability. The noise is forcing your awareness to consciously discern what is real from what is fantasy.

How do I know the impact I make is for the better when I make an effort?

Better is a judgment that often lacks a perspective of the greater whole. Observe. Is there an ease of flow? Are others stirred in their hearts and emotions? Is there life, joy and energy in theirs and in your own as outcomes; or is there chaos, vacuity and desolation?

And the noise?

The noise is a distraction designed to draw your attention. The noise is designed to keep your focus on the human drama and to keep you from seeing the real unfolding behind drawn curtains. The noise is designed to ignite the conflict within you and have you forget your strength comes from the Silence.

As I hear you, the difference I am able to make is empowered by movement in the *silence.* Through my listening for the quiet, I am able to feel the settled places of the real and be inspired to action.

Yes, every action matters. Your very being is action in the greater world. From the air you breathe, to the smile or glare you share, your life is noticed and has value.

I had forgotten and when I sit with *You*, I am reminded. When I share a meal with another, I am reminded. When I share a caring touch, I am reminded. When I share appreciation for a sunrise or a sunset, I am reminded.

There are innumerable sides and channels to engage in. It is your choice which to give your attention to. It is your choice which you choose to feed, to nurture and to harvest. The noise, however, will be there; and it is you who must choose. You must choose whether to engage or, opposingly, to listen to the Silence; to move in the spaces of inspiration and service; and to be held in the care of that which is life giving.

Time and again when I come to *You*, *You* bring me back to the place that my life is of my choosing…

Because it is!

Dear *Teacher,*

Much of my life has been devoted to proving my worth within the context of others. I convinced myself I have to be a faster thinker, a faster performer, a faster producer. Many days are hazy without a record of what my contributions were and if they truly mattered. I am left to question how I measure my own worth if not through the approval of others.

Young One, the notion of worth, as humans have defined it, is enmeshed in the constructs of financial systems, education systems, class systems, religious and familial systems. You have assumed and accepted your worth is inextricably tied to one or many of those systems. Consider who and what you might be in the absence of the delusion that your worth is determined by those systems.

I have great difficulty feeling what my value would be absent from those contexts. I am aware how easily I get caught in the trappings of following the lead of others with little concern for whether their path is to be my own. I have witnessed examples of others walking their own way; and I have not known the preparation, the many failures and successes they experienced as well as the pain and joy of each of their steps. I delude myself into believing I can walk in the same ways they have; I can succeed as they have; and I can experience a fulfilling sense of their value as my own. I flutter from one path to another only to be left with a feeling of emptiness and disappointment in myself.

Disappointment is a symptom of forgetting your essential nature. Disappointment reminds you to listen to your truth if you are willing to hear its teaching.

It becomes increasingly difficult for me, when I am in my disappointment, to hear its message. All I see and hear are failures and echoes of elusive dreams as I measure myself against others.

Have you considered stopping the cycle of assuming another's path; taking on their trajectory as your own; succeeding or failing in reaching the end goal; and still feeling no pleasure in the journey or the accomplishment? Have you considered sitting with your own quiet, unspoken heart's desire; feeling the fullness of your desire's alignment with your own passions; and measuring your success based on each lesson of each step along your own chosen journey?

When I envision my untrodden landscape, I sense opportunities to gather energy and to harness the lessons of each step while holding in my awareness the goal, whatever that may be. There feels to be a sustaining quality and a stability that allows me to not dwell in disappointment. I feel the opportunity to question the missteps with curiosity and neutrality rather than judgment. I feel the opportunity to learn through asking where I can adjust and continue on.

Traveling the path of others that is not your own is exhaustive to your own wellbeing. Walk your own way, feel your own value and savor each.

Young One, may I share a moment with you? You have sought my counsel for days and even years. Still you have yet to commit to your life. You continue to engage in your habits and your patterns that hold you in a place of stasis. You continue to indulge in your distractions and refuse to do the work required for your own growth and maturation. Why?

My *Teacher*, I feel all the reasons I might give are excuses when the truth is, I am stuck in my adolescent desires. I am bound by my desires for the pleasures of my body; bound by the pleasures of my delusions; bound to reasons that blame my circumstances and enable me to not take responsibility for my life.

You are choosing the great sleep. You are waiting to be consumed by all the forces that cause you to deviate from what is your true nature. You are choosing pain and suffering as your teachers.

Your words have merit. When I look back, I can recall with crystal clarity each of my experiences that invoked pain. Those that were genuinely nurturing and supportive were slow to excite and thus left whispering imprints on my memory. I am aware of my craving and addiction to living in imbalance and extremes. Dare I say it is those experiences that would have me feel alive.

But at what cost? How quickly do you bring on loneliness and depression? How quickly do you bring on disease? How quickly do you bring on a premature death, both of the spirit and of the physical body? Your life is precious and finite. There are experiences that excite and are a part of life. It is the imbalance you called out that disconnects you and would have you believe it is only those experiences that give quality to your being.

I have noticed there is a cycle to engaging in my addictions to excitement, whatever their modalities. I notice there is a precipitant, a trigger, that compels me to forgo my better judgments. I get bored, and I take to computer gaming. I get lonely, and I take to sexual encounters. I get worried, and I take to binge eating. I get emotionally hurt, and I take to a drug of choice. There is a moment of excitement in controlling what I am able and engaging in the "high". For brief moments, I forget, and I disconnect. When I come down, I am still left to confront my circumstances. The cycle then begins again.

Does that cycle truly feed you? Does that cycle comfort you? Does that cycle provide you a safety in your being?

It does not. I am embarrassed to be so very exposed before you. This conversation hurts my heart, and I can only cry because I am aware. I cry because I am aware that from this moment forward, I can choose the excitement. I can choose it while also knowing how that excitement will end, only to begin again. My time has run its course, and I can no longer deny what is in my heart. The desire to be and to do better is my task and mine alone.

Dear *Teacher*,

The sun began to set as I made my way along a quiet walk. I felt a deeper connection with the natural world throughout the day and was wrapped in a knowing of safety. As the light began to fade, the blanket of comfort I enjoyed began to fray. I began to notice my thoughts warning me and ushering me to return home. Darkness fell, and I quickened my pace. For much of the evening, I was confronted with my own insecurity and mortality. I recognized my comfort was contingent on what I could see and know. When in darkness, my sight failed. My other, less developed, senses heightened and caused me to startle at the slightest touch or sound.

Young One, humans are insecure by design. They are not the fastest so as to outrun a predator. Nor are they the slowest so as to blend with their environments. They are not the strongest to overpower the mightiest of creatures nor the tallest to see beyond their own limitations. What you do possess is your creativity. It is through creativity you build all manners of comfort to ward off and protect against threats. It is also in your extreme desire for safety that your creativity disconnects you from the natural cycles, to include that of the day and night cycles.

I grew up in suburbia where lights were ever present. And in my youth, I was never acquainted with true darkness. Now I know only fear when wrapped in the nighttime. There felt to be a deep knowing of the imbalance in my relationship to the day and night cycles well before *You* spoke it into my awareness.

That is because there still is that seed each human carries that yearns for harmony. It is a harmony with the natural world that does not deny your frailties but embraces them. It is a harmony that germinates the seed, encouraging its maturation, bringing you into balance with the Earth-Sky relationship and the Day-Night cycles.

There cannot be one without the other; that is true. But, the overwhelming fear I experience in the presence of true darkness paralyzes my want for building a deeper alliance with the night. I do not know how to quiet my fears and to open to the greater harmony.

Young One, you began in the womb, in the darkness. It is only your creative mind that has convinced you that you do not know.

How do I begin to reclaim my relationship to the darkness and to the night?

Begin with your fear. Acknowledge its gift in serving as a warning to alert you to real dangers and not to your frights of the unknowns. Ask of your fear to walk with you in allegiance instead of igniting your bodily senses and spurring you to run at the slightest shadow. Walk from the lighted spaces to the progressive, darker spaces building your love for the night energies and all that they offer. Allow the night's wisdoms to unfold in your heart. With time your love for the night will grow and you will feel an even greater safety and harmony than you have ever known.

Dear *Teacher,*

I have been sitting with our last conversation of maturing into all that I am able to be. What is becoming evident is the fragility of my discipline and my practices. I consistently waiver between starts and stops in my practice only to frustrate my growth. I see little evidence of progress, and I am left with the question, "What is the purpose?"

You are experiencing a point of inflection. For each moment, there is a test of your resolve to change. Your current moment is no different

My struggle is with intimacy. It is intimacy that is reliant upon my willingness to speak to what is in my heart. There is a great ease in my ability when there is love, affection and adoration that live there. Yet when there is potential for conflict, my words are restrained. I hear my internal, young one reminding me of our history and of the pain we experienced when we spoke our truth. In those moments, I shied away from engaging in conflict, shut down my emotions' expressions and closed away my heart. I convinced myself that the conflict had no value if at risk was a shaking of my foundation of safety.

There is never, and never will be, expression without conflict. Conflict involves risk to mental, physical and even emotional safety. What you are speaking to is the latter. You risk rejection even in your desire to share your love with another. Yet you are empowered in the knowing that the risk, the internal conflict, is worthy of expressing for the opportunity of knowing the outcome of that expression. You, equally, convince yourself that when there is the potential for emotional hurt, engaging in the conflict has no value. I challenge you to review your relationships and the moments you chose not to engage in conflicts. What were the outcomes?

The conflict's catalyst lay in wait. It slept unresolved until another moment arose to awaken that conflict. Only, the second time, there was an amplification that was compounded by the original unresolved moment.

Continue to track your pattern. What then?

Emotionally, I disengage. The conflict sleeps. I forget about the moment. I am triggered once more. The cycle begins again with greater intensity. I explode when at my emotional capacity. At its climax the relationship is dissolved, unrepairable from having been built upon moments of unresolved conflict. I convince myself that my life is to be spent traveling alone with another never truly knowing the depths of my being.

And you are never alone. You will always be in relationship as a part of a Greater Whole. By not embracing your full expression, to include giving voice to when you feel slighted, feel hurt, you rob not only yourself of the opportunity to deepen your relationships, but you rob others of knowing you truly. How lonely of a place that will continue to be for you to reside. Are you willing to engage in the conflict, in the risk, in order to walk in the deeper knowing? Only you can answer that question for you.

Dear *Teacher*,

I have a bit of fear putting to paper these conversations I have had with *You*. The fear I carry is based in the backlash that I have observed from others. Those proclaiming to have the one truth often perpetuate the backlash. I acknowledge I cannot speak to what is true for another. I can say I have a knowing that *truth* spans cultures, backgrounds and experiences.

Young One, truth does cross cultures and peoples. There is a resonance that speaks to the shared experience of humankind. Humans, through the ages, have experienced inspiration from sunrises and sunsets and the magnificence of the colors they share. Humans have dreamed big dreams that have changed the course and trajectory of many lives. The truth in those experiences is that there is a Universal Creative Principle that humans engage with be it consciously or not.

Then why is there so much violence? Why do we cling so fiercely to our experience of what is *truth*?

Truth manifests through many gateways and humans have a very limited capacity for recognizing when they are in the presence of truth because of the limitations of their physical vessels. Still, truth, the Universal Creative Principle is called many things: Science, God, Gaia, The Void to name a few. The violence is based in a fear that would challenge the foundation of who and what humans have known themselves to be and a need to reconcile their self-perception with discordant experiences.

The conclusion I would have to consider is I can't possibly know the totality of *truth* but can only recognize when I am in its presence. My own life's path would force me to reflect on the frustrations of my lived experiences; in that, I have held the expectation of a linear experience to explain fleeting moments of engagement with the *Universal Creative Principle*. I am forced to concede each moment was but a single heartbeat in time.

If but a heartbeat, arrogance would have you profess to know All, and arrogance would shatter your innocence of wonder. Arrogance steals you away from truth and abandons you in fields barren of connection.

…tilling infertile soil. It is only through wonder that I am able to feel into the *Universal Creative Principle* not to understand but to be in the influence of *Its* being.

Each moment of wonder is a gift, an invitation, to open to a different perspective of the Universal Creative Principle. In your heart and being begins to grow a rich quality of meaning and relationship to the Whole.

If living in wonder, I would not need to fight or to profess my truth as the *truth*. Rather, I engender my heart with an openness, a curiosity, to experience *truth* through another's experience. There is a relief that feels to be washing over and through me with this awareness. There feels to be a closer-ness to *truth*. Thank you.

Dear *Teacher,*

I want to be a doctor. I want to be a firefighter. I want to be a military officer were the many answers I responded with to the question of who and what I wanted to be when I grew up. The last of which propelled me into unplanned futures. The military forced me to reconnect with my own and my family's agendas. And so began, decades of errors, decades of deconstruction and decades of pain in my re-discovery of me.

Young One, you spent much of your development living and being the right persona for others. You were the nice son, the young man that minded his tongue, and the one who chose not to disturb the waters of normed behavior even when doing so fractured your truth. The habitual shearing of your parts to fit the assumptions and expectations of others could only result in pain. The pain is the result of the weight from carrying others' perceptions of you and you assimilating them as your own. The pain is the crushing contortions you spent your life molding yourself into out of a desire for acceptance and survival.

Truth. Much of the time I spent rambling directionless. The burden of maintaining others' perceptions requires, in every moment, all-consuming energy. Consumption of my physical, consumption of my mental and emotional, consumption of my spiritual and inspirational beings left little remaining to be my essential self.

The burdens will be crushing if you allow them to be so. Deconstruction is painful when ripping the faux grafts from your own being. Only through continued, focused and finer excisions can discovery of your essential self be revealed. And through your process, what have you come to know about you?

I discovered a depth-fullness of compassion that I readily gave to others yet fell woefully short in extending to myself the same grace. I discovered a capacity to bear my own hurts in isolation while feeling the need to salve others'. I discovered a bridled humor awaiting full expression.

It is in your humor that you were able to counterbalance your pain. It is in your humor that you were able to listen to your essential self reflecting to your consciousness the discord. It is in your humor that you were able to peak into your essential self and allow micro-moments of light to radiate through the gaps.

What occurs to me is how worthy it has been to feel pain, to exhale, to inquire, to laugh, to learn and to start again. There is a quality to self-discovery that fills me with appreciation for all that has been, is and will be.

You are touching into the gift that is life. Your life is not inconsequential, and it matters. The spark that is you can only be expressed through you, and to bury you under the weight of others' agendas is to extinguish your spark.

That's to say I am not complete with excising, uncovering, me; and I do know I will not stop.

Dear One,

would you sit with me while I share a story with you? It is of your life through My eyes. Your origin began long before the life you now incarnate. Two beings, your mother and father, knew not of your coming into being. The path they chose was one of love, lust, power and survival. Your father was not yet ready to receive you as he tried to reconcile who and what he wanted to be in a disapproving culture of the black man. Your mother stood by him until his demons ignited your mother's protector instincts. She chose to nurture your life and to go beyond his violence. As a child no more than a year old and unable to yet give words to your experience, you heard the shouting, saw the violence and felt the pain of your parents, one as the victim and the other — victimizer.

As you grew, your own voice was still quiet. You spoke only when necessary. You observed. You listened with an intention beyond your years. You felt your pain and the pain of others as your own. You would twitch and seize without warning. One hospital visit, two and more. Fighting to claim your place and your life, you grew and overcame the fits. You put up boundaries, shutting off your sensitivities to others.

Yet you could not shut them out completely. The man shot and bleeding before you shocked your senses back to feeling. You patched the fracture and went on. The man stabbed on the street brought, again, to your awareness a knowing that you have an unavoidable compassion. And still you tarred the gap and went on. The mother and daughter struck by the bus shook your foundation and still you went on.

You began to listen. You shed the expectations others had of you that you held as your own. You stepped into a new place of inquiry, a place that began to force you to redefine you. You began to chisel, one stone at a time, to create a space and a place where compassion could reside.

You touched into the healing arts that opened you to a greater depth of sensitivity. You felt the gross and fine pains that others carried. You moved their ailments, brought them relief and greater balance. You deeply felt in your own being a gratitude for another's trust and willingness to give you an opportunity to serve in a way you had not, until those moments, considered.

It is a blessing to be of service however I am able. It is a responsibility I do not take lightly.

There is still more to discover. You have more learning. You have more growing. You have more serving. As you do so, you have a responsibility to pass on what you have learned. Your life will also come to an end and the journey of the young ones will begin. It is your responsibility to prepare them for what is to come. You cannot hold that responsibility alone. It is shared. There are those, though, who are not aware they also have a part in passing on the knowledge earned. Part of that knowledge is there is a compassion that goes beyond humankind. It is one that enables all things to be all they can be. You are but at the tip of its embodiment. Through your own lived experiences, share your compassion so others may feel into their own.

Dear *Teacher,*

I have been curious about why I am able to so vividly recall some past experiences and yet so little of others. It makes sense to me the most memorable ones are those that held me the most emotionally engaged. I can't help but wonder if those that I am unable to call to memory held little emotional imprinting and therefore held little value.

Young One, your emotions bring many blessings with them while still having the capacity to wreak havoc when unchecked or unexpressed in balanced, useful ways. Your emotions, when at their height, evoke a memory of your experience. Often in those moments, you are unaware of your decision point. The decision is to process what you are able to in that moment and allow your emotions to cycle in their natural way, or to hold on to that moment in time. It is the holding on that then is carried with you for many days, months and years.

I can't help but see how the two ways memories imprint and how their experiences leave us revolving around the intensities of our emotions. At the extreme end of the spectrum, however, there is memory loss.

Of course.

Would *You* be able to share with me the mechanics of how we engage with traumatic experiences within the context of our ability or inability to process them in the moment?

First, let's be clear by what you mean by traumatic experience. Trauma may take two forms in which there is great harm to your body or great harm to your emotional being. Often there is a combination of the two that creates the total landscape of the traumatic experience itself. The trauma necessitates a response that can be distilled to three outcomes. You can forget the experience and truly have no memory of it. Doing so is a defense to enable you to live a functional life. Though, the unmanaged trauma will still manifest in ways that you may not be aware of nor be able to track back to the original trauma. The second response is the imprint and where the pain of the experience is assumed as your identity. You remember and hold onto the trauma with resentment, with anger, and little joy finds its way into your lived experiences from the moment of the original trauma forward. The last response is when you are aware there is freedom to be gained in being with the trauma. This is not a being with the trauma in a way that is reengaging with the trauma, but in a way that allows a space of understanding of its appropriate place in your life. Being with the trauma allows you to process the pain, build an alliance with it and be taught by it.

It feels as if I would be able to share with others my own process with the hope they too would be able to find theirs. There is also a sense that the memory, its intensity, does not have to be held on to or even recalled in its entirety to be of benefit.

Every part of the experience may hold a teaching for you even if there are only fragments.

Young One,

there is much change coming. The times before you will bring unrest, uncertainty, pain and grief. There will be great losses both of humans and of the natural world. Many warnings have been given, and still there is human denial. There is a refusal to grow beyond your own clutching to past and present patterns of destruction. It is not too late.

My *Teacher, Your* words have made me uneasy once more. I have worked to be better each day than I was the day before. I fall short, feel failure and self-judgment. I then have difficulty attaining self-forgiveness. I question what it is I have to offer that is of value, and I fall prey to the negativity that would have me believe I have none.

Your value is granted at the moment of your birth. You have unique gifts and talents that can only be expressed through you. It is for you to give life in each moment to your original blessing.

How do I do that while recognizing the unrest to come?

The unrest in the greater world may undo your inner world, most assuredly, should you not do the work to maintain your center. You know your value by going into the quiet of your being. Listening to the guidance that comes only while in that space, brings forth a calibration with the Sacred. That alignment emboldens you with the certainty that you are safe in your being. In your safety, you bring forth the fullness of you and thus your value.

It is challenging to follow the simplicity in your guidance. My days are bombarded with my priorities to work, to family, to friends, to the maintenance and upkeep of my basic needs. How do I find space to go within and to listen when the time I have is short?

Your priorities are set by you and you alone. How you choose to spend your time is a reflection of what you deem most important. Do you prioritize your work over your basic needs? Do you prioritize your family above your work? Do you prioritize your inner work and alignment above all else to guide you in how to serve in a balanced way? All those are for you to decide.

It sounds to me that my value is also enmeshed in what I prioritize.

Because it is. Your sense of value gets challenged when your priorities run in conflict with who you know your true self to be.

The sense I feel when I direct my priority and focus inward for guidance is a culling of what is misaligned. There is a falling away of detrimental relation-ships, toxic behaviors, destructive patterns, and a settling into new ways of being. As an outcome, the value I feel is in my growth, in my humility, and as *You* said, in my expression of the fullness of me.

Listening in the Quiet, listening for the guidance of the Sacred and that of the natural world will lead you back to you. It is you who must decide whether or not to hear them.

Dear *Teacher,*

I have been reviewing the circles of relations throughout my life. There are many that stand out as they have come and gone or withstood the challenges of time. There is one, with my sister, that feels incomplete with parts left undone. I don't quite know when it began. Nor do I fully understand its genesis. We were inseparable as adolescents. We found ourselves making different choices and growing in different directions as we matured. I am left wondering why.

Young One, your relationships are reflections of who you are and choose to be in each moment. This truth includes those born with you in blood and those whom you attract. There are agreements, conscious or not, that are made that hold the relationship together or move it to dissolution. Each relationship is designed to support a process of growth and learning. Those lessons are far and wide.

The act or notion that agreements bind relationships is not something I have always been aware of, but there is the sense that the reasons we enter into those contracts is out of an expectation of some reward.

The agreements are not always spoken. They may be expressed as loyalty to another. The agreement to stay in a relationship because it is expected may offer a reward of maintaining stability. An agreement may present as fear of change with an equal reward of stability. An agreement may show as support for another person's strengths with the reward manifesting as an empowerment of them being all they can be.

How I understand agreements is they may be beneficial or problematic. They may be beneficial, in that the agreement was entered into with conscious intent. All those involved receive mutual support that improves the wellbeing of all that may be expressed physically, mentally, emotionally or spiritually. An environmental activist may protest the destruction of waterways. The benefit would not only be for humans' access to clean water but also for all the natural critters that would be reliant upon those waterways. Conversely, it may be problematic, in that the agreement creates power dynamics of zero-sum experiences. One must necessarily lose in the experience for the other to be the clear winner and beneficiary at the expense of the first. As exampled, a wife may abuse a husband to affirm her dominance.

There is a caution in your understanding. Beneficial and problematic are constructs that point to a perspective that would absolve the participants of the lessons they are to learn. Agreements all have the power to teach and to strengthen alignment with the natural flow of all things. That is the goal.

The relationship with my sister feels unfinished, and the lessons I would learn with her would come to me in other relationships. The lessons in setting healthy boundaries, honest communications and building intimacy with emotional vulnerability are ever present. My lessons are mine, and the circles I inhabit will bring them forth.

Dear *Teacher,*

I shared that my relationship with my sister was broken. I am reminded of *Your* teaching and guiding me in knowing that relationships have a purpose. Once that purpose has been served, the relationship evolves, transforms or comes to an end. There is still this feeling that my sister's and my relationship is not yet complete.

Young One, what you are experiencing is unresolved thoughts and feelings. What you are experiencing is all that has been unsaid and all that has been undone.

Though that may be true, how do I bring closure so as to lay to rest the unresolved? How do I let go of the hurt and free that space occupied by my unfulfilled desire?

Once that place in your heart has held deep emotion for another such as love, there is created a memory. The memory and experience is unique to you. The hurt you reference does not die. As you sit with the hurt and its lessons, the hurt settles. The hurt is heard and validated. The hurt, then, is willing to align with you as your teacher and support you in relationships yet to unfold. Listening is the way to resolution. Resolution does not always equate to feeling good. Resolution is an act of creating wholeness in your own being. No one can bring you to resolution other than you.

I feel I have sat with my hurt. I have listened, and it feels like a continual process. What more may I do to bring greater resolution to this relationship?

Write. Though the words may never be received by your sister, the act of writing your thoughts and feelings opens you to a deeper knowing. That is but one way to resolution; and yes, it is a process. Resolution is a practice that requires no less than your full commitment to your own healing.

My sister, it has taken me many years to acknowledge my part in the broken circle of our relationship. I was filled with such self-doubt that I believed, for many years, my actions impacted no one other than me. I was self-absorbed in my pain. Very little allowed me to take notice of the importance I held for others and what I meant to them or them to me. I felt only the need to escape. I imagine you have believed, these many years, that I abandoned you. For that, I am sorry. I can't pretend to know your challenges. I can't pretend any longer or even absolve myself of the hurt I caused you. I doubt there will come a time when I will know the true why behind us having had nothing more than silence between us. I do know that the blessing I wish for you is a long life filled with much joy. May you find other circles that nurture, care and support you in your journey. May you always be held safe in your Creator's care. And may your life be good.

That is a good blessing. As you send forth your prayer, notice the space of resolve you have just opened to. That space of resolution will not manifest without sincerity of heart and intention. Notice, the practice of resolution goes beyond your mind. Resolution is active. Resolution is emotional. Resolution is living…always.

Dear *Teacher*,

Today I experienced what I have felt many times — invisible. Sitting with a friend, I was reminded that my life is inconsequential to some. There was a young man who came to visit for a while, and my presence was not acknowledged though I greeted him. I was left with my insecurities on full display, questioning what I had done and why I had been dismissed.

Young One, I hear your wanting to be validated by another. You and I have shared in discussions that your validation may never be propped up and supported by what others think or don't think, say or don't say to you. Those moments are reminders to strengthen within you a knowing and alignment with the natural order of all things.

But, I am a social creature with feelings. I don't see how I will be completely free of caring what others think, say and feel about me. I cannot pretend the moments when I feel dismissed are non-impactful to my sensitive self.

It is right to acknowledge you will feel hurt. What matters is that you allow the emotion to pass through you and not define you. What matters is the learning and the dissolution of the hurt to keep your own space of compassion open.

It is easy to shutter my heart and expression. I know that pattern far too well, and it is a lonely way to experience my life. I would extend myself with an agenda of reciprocity. My giving was not done freely. When what I expected in return was not born out, I felt anger and resentment. I question why I should reach out to others if not reciprocated.

When you open yourself fully to your life, you open to the great, unknowable Mystery. When you close yourself, so too do you close yourself to the wondrous. Though you may feel dismissed, when you are open and are able to give freely, you are then able to see

There have been times I have engaged in dismissing another. Walking by a man on the street covered in soil, I turned a blind eye. I did not want to know what he wanted from me. I made assumptions I would be asked for money, for food, for drugs. Few times have I taken the time to truly see him. I came to *You* asking about my hurt fueled by feeling a victim. And, *You* have shown me there are many complexities to my being that are engaged in dynamic exchanges. I have been the victim, on one hand, and the other — the perpetrator.

To believe you can know yourself in totality is a posture in true arrogance. You, like all that is around, are an experiment. Your task is to probe, to inquire and to hold yourself with reverent curiosity.

I suspect doing so opens to greater non-judgment of myself and that of others and dare I say — freedom.

Dear *Teacher*,

Would you be willing to sit with me and to witness my process? In my time of meditation this morning, I was made aware that I have extended forgiveness and grace to many but have not fully done so to me. I have had moments of atoning for my self-abuse and self-neglect. I realize I still have yet more to do as I discover the aspects of my being I have abandoned.

Young One, you are discovering and listening to all that makes you, you. As you cannot know the fullness of another being, so too must you continue exploring your different parts. The parts you favor are carried in your conscious awareness. Those you do not are walled in your unconscious. Only when those parts have cordoned your attention through discomfort, dis-ease, do you pay attention. You are learning to hear their subtle calls and to give them an audience so that they may be embraced as an alliance rather than adversary. Who is it, within, that has called you to make amends?

My Magical Child shared I am not yet done in rebuilding trust with him. I must be continually listening for the wisdom that he has earned that brought me into adulthood. And so, I say to him:

I have looked at old photographs and met your eyes with contempt. I saw anger and deadness reflected back at me. I saw a person I wanted to forget. I remembered times I judged you and asked you why you were not smarter, why you were not more physically strong and why you were so emotionally vulnerable. Many of those times I could have done well to stop, to not continue on and to end my living. What stopped me was my fear as it was greater than my resolve. Even now I feel the uneasiness of how little I regarded your strength and creativity with which you engaged in our life to keep us going. I am so sorry. I am sorry for forgetting you and abandoning you. I am sorry for closing out the light of joy and gratitude all those times you needed me. I welcome your sensitivities as I know now it is a gateway to feeling life in its fullness. I welcome your wisdom and truth so that we may travel together from this place forward.

Resolution continues in every moment. As I have witnessed your proclamation, you are now accountable to stopping and listening to your Magical Child when he wishes to speak. You are responsible for considering his guidance, negotiating with him in those moments, and coming to consensus for how to go on.

He is saying to me he will no longer be quiet in the recesses of my unconscious as he too has the right to live fully in the now. As I take his hand and usher him from the times, places and spaces he was left alone, he is welcomed in my here and now. I will not let go.

What more does he have to share with you?

He feels he belongs, embraced in knowing we are yet again connecting and building a stronger, unfrayed, tether. He says to me we still have much work before us. He offers me his laughter, and I am comforted in the lightness, the music, the magic of his being.

One, two, three, four generations back, and there stops the clarity of my blood-line. Coursing through me are unknown faces, unknown histories and no known lands to call home. Dear *Teacher*, how am I to honor my lineage when I feel unrooted and disconnected from my people?

True, many of your bloodline were ripped from your native lands, your ancestral homes, Young One. True, the natural cycles of many of those lives were extinguished well before their due time. Equally true is that many survived. If it were not so, you would not be.

I have to acknowledge I still feel unsettled even though I do live. I feel uneasy not knowing where I came from or to where I am headed. There is this desire that I also want to celebrate traditions, to sing and dance the songs of my an-cients. The languages, the stories, the imagery and the fullness of how my an-cestors lived, died when they did. What was handed down was pain as well as memories of grief and suffering.

If this is your conclusion, you have not yet dug deep enough. When you listen deeply, the songs and stories are carried in your laughter, in your joy and in your ability to forgive. They are carried in the connections your ancestors held not just with the lands they inhabited but with the Earth herself. Your ancestors imprinted in you how to con-nect to all that you share your existence with. Knowledge is never lost though it may be forgotten. Look to the natural world. Not only have humans been displaced of their own doing or of disaster, but so too have the non-humans. And they survived.

Humancentrism is an affliction. I do not often consider examples from nature of how to be, how to survive, and how to thrive. There are countless examples of destruction of habitats and still the critters adapt and continue on. For them, there is only now in time. I notice they cannot be anything other than what they are. Therein lies the imprint of their histories.

And how do they honor their history?

They listen to the sacred knowing within their own beingnesses. They live each moment with intention and fulfill their purpose for which they were brought into existence. When I touch the true me, I feel a knowing of that which makes me, me. I have joy and strength. I have a gift of seeing patterns and working with those patterns in beneficial ways. I also have insecurities and capacities to work with creative energies in destructive or benevolent ways. When I am living my purpose, I am honoring my ancestors though I may not know their names.

You are connected to not only your blood ancestors but to All. When you are in your fullness, all beings are glad. They acknowledge you as a human truly being. They do so in acknowledging your equality rather than dominance.

I forget my part in the *whole*. I shall honor all that is by being of service in all I can be. I feel their spirits. They cry with my pain. They dance when I dance. They sing when I sing. They rejoice when I am in my fullness.

Dear *Teacher,*

I feel *Your* presence around me though I am not always consciously aware. When I am emotional, unbalanced and clouded in my direction, *You* are there waiting for me to open myself to receiving your counsel. I come to you now with gratitude and humility— seeking. I can't help but question if what I seek deeper meaning in exists only in my hopes and dreams. I question if there is any meaning to my experiences.

Young One, your faith in there being a purpose to all things has been unwavering. Why now does it stumble?

There are many times I feel my day is spent mundanely working, mundanely attending to my basic needs, mundanely chattering with other humans and mundanely starting the process over with each new day. Rarely in those moments do I feel moved or inspired.

That is a consequence of the limits to how you experience and define what is inspiring. You have the expectation that the Earth shakes, the thunder roars, the stars burn iridescent and bright in every moment to get your attention and to shock your awareness to forces greater than your own. The meaning, the inspiration, is in the quality of subtle vibrations that go unnoticed in your daily experience. The subtle goes unnoticed because you have not yet trained and practiced yourself to hear.

How do I train when I have engaged in creativity with my hands by your advice? How do I train when I have sat in the *silence* at your guidance? How do I practice when I have walked in the natural spaces at your counsel? I have done all those, and still, I arrive at a place of questioning.

True you have done all those and you have grown. Your maturation is not yet done, however, and will never be. You, we, are all — always — in progress. I direct you now to ask what has been the quality of the time you have spent in your practice. Have the times you have engaged been ones of routine? Or, have those times had a quality in each experience of being alive, living and breathing?

I, disappointingly, must own they have been very different with the balance towards a quality of not truly engaging in the process.

Now consider expecting to find a greater number of inspirational moments when your discipline to your practice is inconsistent in the micro-experiences. You cannot notice the subtle if each of those experiences are not themselves honored as sacred and inspirational.

My mind would call me to question the purpose of the *All*. I spiral, unchecked, into feelings of grief and anger. My task, then, is to regard each moment consciously. Honor the forces and alliances at work in humble exchanges. I am to find inspiration in every breath, in every word spoken, and in every action chosen. I am to notice the subtle, to welcome their wisdom and to allow them to move around, in and through me. And, I am inspired.

Dear *Teacher,*

More often than not, I am absorbed in my own life and circumstances. Then I witness an amazing example of care and compassion being extended from one person to another. A husband was so gentle and patient with his wife as she moved only as quickly as her body would allow her. She had several moments of instability. Yet, he paced alongside her ensuring her safety. I was reminded we each have a pace in our lives, and we must take notice of what is most important.

Young One, you have just brushed against the universal law of humility that holds no thing, no one, is any greater or any lesser than another. You witnessed a demonstration of honoring another's life. The husband performed his service in supporting his wife with willingness and attentiveness. He, too, receives the blessing of knowing he is contributing to his wife's quality of life which might be far different if it were not for him.

I've not been a caregiver and cannot pretend to know the impact of the negotiations, the sacrifices and the blessings that come from partnership in that way. I question if I would have the capacity to have the depths of patience needed to be a provider. I question if I could maintain healthy exchanges as a caregiver and ward against co-dependencies. I question how I would maintain my care and devotion to improving the quality of life of whomever I would be entrusted with for their care.

Caregiving requires compromise. More so, it takes vigilance to maintain your self-identity so as to not be consumed by the duties of caregiving or care receiving. Honest communication is a requirement for that balance. Too often honest communication can be silenced out of a desire to protect one's self from pain or hurt. The short-term result may be conflict free with, however, the compounded silence culminating in explosive exchanges causing more harm long term.

I have known cruelty doesn't equate to honest communication and honesty can be given with compassion. I can't help but question, also, what happens when the care receiver or caregiver dies. What happens to the other? Even contemplating the question, I sense a deep sadness for those whose identities were intertwined with the other.

What you are attuning to is the loss of relationship. That is not unique to caregiving and care receiving relationships. The sadness is for the loss of life that is precious and appropriate for mourning. What you witnessed was a blessing that awakened you to a different way of relating to your sphere of life. Yours does not always afford you the chance to know in that way. Let the blessing in and let it fill you with gladness for another's process having moved you.

I am moved and awed that such a seemingly simple gesture cracked open a seed in my awareness and has inspired in me a feeling of gratitude — gratitude for being at that place in time, gratitude for witnessing a process unfold and gratitude for being able to recognize a miracle before me.

Dear *Teacher,*

This morning I sat in contemplation of what the day may bring. It was brought to my attention how much resistance I have to change. Truly, I delude myself in believing I am open to new experiences, new perspectives and new ways of being. When in actuality, change elicits fear in me of which I am not always aware. That fear manifests thoughts that say to me, "I was not interested in the experience. It was too hard. I don't have time." Then I criticize myself for missing a chance to have a rich experience.

Young One, change is not always easy, and outcomes that are pleasant to you are not always guaranteed. Life, itself, is never certain. All of our experiences bring with them a chance to learn and to grow even when there is pain.

I feel that is what scares me most — the prospect of evoking self-inflicted pain by jumping into the unknown.

By giving way to your fear in every instance of an opportunity to experience newness, you also rob yourself of possible and unexpected joys. Yes, you have a fragile body that feels pain, and it has its own wisdom. You have a creative, analytical mind that can help discern true danger from illusionary potentials.

I am not confident in knowing whether or not I have built the bridges between my parts. I am not confident in knowing if they are aligned and in agreement in wanting to engage in the experiences. I am not confident in knowing that if they are in agreement in their wants that they are in agreement, as well, in knowing how to proceed.

Begin simply. Ask your mind what it needs. What brings it joy? What causes it distress? Ask your body and emotional being the same. Where are the commonalities?

Where are the differences? Where are the places of dissonance? The last is equally as important in knowing since that is where the fractures between your parts may occur.

And if I am able to become aware of the dissonance, how do I make peace within?

Choose physical representations for your mind, for your body and for your emotions. Introduce them, one at a time, to each other. Ask them where they have caused harm to one another. Ask them what it will take to build trust and what they each can commit to in building that trust. Acknowledge to yourself the process will need practice. With authentic engagement in the process, you will begin to notice greater alignment between them and the dissonance quiets over time.

They, then, work together to provide greater clarity and discernment of what is before me. I can choose more powerfully the experiences I engage in with intention rather than choosing, by default, out of fear. *You* have said the process will require practice. I am willing to work at that process and recognize it may be a lifelong practice. I can't help but feel it will be, and is, worth it.

QUESTIONS TO CONSIDER
WHILE ENGAGING WITH EACH READING

Of Self

1. What were your physical responses to the reading? Did you notice your pulse racing? Did you notice a sense of body relaxation? Did you notice physical aches or sensations that were general or localized?
2. What have been your emotions' responses to the reading? Were you angry, elated, joyous, saddened, fearful? What were the triggers to the emotional response?
3. Were your own experiences validated or not? Why or why not?
4. What thoughts or memories were recalled, and what lessons do they have for you?
5. Who does the Teacher represent for you and your life? Who and what are your teachers?
6. How might you open yourself more to seeing you without judgment?
7. What do you need to do to invite in more self-forgiveness?
8. What recurring experiences have you had, and what do you feel the lesson is they are collectively trying to share with you?
9. If you were to die at this moment, what would be left undone, unsaid, unexpressed?
10. How are you living your true self and expression, or what stops you?
11. How have your experiences shaped your perspective of who and what you are?
12. How have you contributed to the betterment of your environment: your body, your home, your community, and your natural surroundings?

Of Other

1. Is there any amends that need to be made and if so to whom?
2. What is your legacy, your contribution?
3. How would you describe or discover Universal Laws?

SETTING AND WORKING WITH A SACRED SPACE

Setting a sacred space begins with intention. For the sacred space to be one of clarity and beneficial exchange, there must be humility as a necessity. True humility is placing oneself as equal to all that is and acknowledging that all things have wisdom from which we may learn. We are no greater and no lesser than any other. When we are able to be in humility, we are able to discern when we are in the presence of *wisdom*. We are better able to distinguish *wisdom* from our own imaginings, hopes and wishes for situations to be different than they are. If we are unable to be in humility, we position ourselves to succumb to delusion or illusion. We set ourselves up to falter in setting the sacredness of the space we are working with. The space we set will hold whatever intention we bring, be it conscious or not.

Sacred spaces are what enables you to contact the *silence*. This may be done in the middle of New York City or in the sanctums of Mesa Verde. Begin with, consciously acknowledging you are about to engage in a sacred practice. That may be amplified by beginning with deep breathing for thirty seconds to one minute to orient your mind to your body experience. Doing so begins to quiet the mental noise and position you for greater receptivity. Each action will contribute to the creation of that sacred space. You may consider lightning a candle. Do so with respect and intention for its contributions to the sacred space. You may choose a music track that is consistent in its rhythm and vocals. Do so with reverence and gratitude for its contribution. You may consider creating a spot to hold representations for the *Teacher* you are working with or more generally those that help you relax into the *silence*.

The space is set once there feels to be a shift in the environment around and within you. Take notice of your body. Is there greater ease, slowed breathing, decreased stress and anxiety? How have your thoughts shifted? Are there less than when you began setting your sacred space? Notice your emotions. Is there a greater sense of safety?

Call on the *Teacher* you wish to work with. Allow your words to be spoken from the heart. It is from the place of sincerity that your *Teacher* will be able to receive your call. An example may be, "Dear *Teacher*. It is my desire to learn more and to be a better human in my life. Would you be with me now and share with me my frailties?" You may choose to use the explicit name of the *Teacher* you are working with which is encouraged.

Allow your *Teacher* to reflect back to you responses to your question. They may not come in the form of words. They may be in images. They may be in sounds, in smells or in tastes. Take note of the sensory responses and how they resonate in your body. It is in your body's response that you know you have received a true response from your *Teacher* rather than your mind working to convince you your experience was real. Ask any clarifying questions you may have throughout. As the experience is coming to a close, ask "What else would you have to share with me?"

Finally, give your heartfelt thanks to your *Teacher* for the willingness to share with you in your exchange. Give thanks to the sacred space and all of the tools that volunteered in helping you to set that space. Release the space and allow the experience to live in you as it will.

QUESTIONS TO ASK WHEN COMMUNING WITH YOUR TEACHER

1. We may often default to assuming the teacher that we have chosen or one that has chosen us is human. I encourage you, when engaging with these questions, to consider expanding your definition of teacher. Teachers may be people, indeed, but they may also be your favorite hiking trail. The *Teacher* may be your favorite type of bird or plant. The most important consideration is remembering that all things have *wisdom*.

2. Who are you? What is your name?

3. Have you been known by other names and in other cultures or traditions?

4. Who and what do you serve?

5. Where are you from?

6. How may I deepen my relationship with you?

7. Why are you willing to work with me?

8. What do you expect of me in our exchange?

9. Have you and I known each other before?

10. Why have you come to me at this time in my life and what is it you are teaching me?

11. How long are we to work together?

12. How do you experience fear, grief, anger, love and joy? What invokes each of these experiences?

13. How will I know when I am in your presence?

14. How do you prefer I call on you for guidance?

15. What are your sacred lessons that you are learning, and how do I contribute to that learning?

16. When is the most meaningful time of day, time of month and season of the year to commune with you?

17. What are some barriers I may encounter in receiving your message clearly, and how do I minimize those barriers?

18. What types of environments would contribute to my ability to hear and experience you more clearly?